Preface

This book is an English version of the panel exhibit "The Truth of the A-bombings and World War II".

As a result of World War II, 3,200,000 precious Japanese lives were lost because of the Japanese government's policy of sending its soldiers and citizens as settler groups to mainland China, Southeast Asia, the various Pacific Islands, and other countries. Many lives were also lost in the bombing of the major cities of Japan by the U.S. forces, in the Battle of Okinawa, and in the atomic bombings of Hiroshima and Nagasaki.

However, for many years after the war, due to their various circumstances, the survivors of the Hiroshima and Nagasaki atomic bombings and other war victims were not able to talk about the horrors they had undergone. This exhibit is therefore the fruit of the persistence of many brave people who, despite the pressure exerted to conceal the truth, persistently delved into the experiences of the survivors and the courageous acts of those who stared to talk about the truth in the hope that a peaceful future will be possible.

This exhibit has been shown all over Japan and has impacted the younger generations who know almost nothing about the horrors of the war. In all places where this exhibit has been shown, many people have been moved. This has become a strong driving force towards their determination to establish a peaceful society and to prevent war from ever occurring again.

This annual exhibit held in Hiroshima City every August summarizes the war experiences of the Japanese people and their hopes for peace. It has steadily spread as a movement and in recent years, many people visiting Hiroshima from different countries around the world have been moved while viewing the exhibits. In translating these panels into English, we would like to spread to the whole world our vision of preventing a similar occurrence of the war experienced by and inflicted by the Japanese people.

Last but not least, we hope that many people around the world will read this report and that it will reinforce a shared international desire for peace in the world.

July, 2017

The Secretariat of the Shimonoseki A-bomb Exhibition

Table of Contents

The Truth of World War II 3
War Survivors' Revelations, on the Basis of Their Experiences

U.S. Air Raids on Japanese Cities 29
Testimonies gathered in various places by the National
Campaign Caravan for the Atomic Bomb Exhibition

The Truth about the Battle of Okinawa 45
The real experiences of 1,000 Okinawans
who suffered during the battle

Atomic Bombs and Poems of Sankichi Toge 52
An Appeal of All Voices from under the Atomic cloud

Defeat – the War Ended at Last 95
Why were as many as 3.2 million people killed?

Japan Became a Center of World Peace Movement 111
The Movement Against Atomic and
Hydrogen Bombs Began
in the Peace Struggle of August 6, 1950

The Truth of World War II

War Survivors' Revelations, on the Basis of Their Experiences

A Japanese soldier carries a wounded comrade in arms on his back on a road to Xuzhou in China. (June 1938)

People Became Poor and War Drew Near

The Economic bubble burst after World War I and depression struck Japan

Children trying to stave off their hunger with uncooked radish in northern part of Japan where the harvest was very bad.

Depositors rushed to a bank which went bankrupt. (Tokyo, 1929)

Official counseling center for selling out daughter. (Yamagata Prefecture)

"A coup attempt was made in Japan after the Manchurian Incident (Japanese invasion of Manchuria in 1931). There were 2,000 cases of peasants' revolts in a single year because the farming villages were stricken by the deep economic crisis. Social unrest could easily be provoked.

At that time, silkworm culture was promoted by the government. Girls began working at silk or spinning mills after completing elementary school. I saw such girls in my village too. They were put in dormitories. That was also a way to reduce the number of mouths their parents had to feed. The girls brought a considerable sum of money home when they visited on summer holidays. If not, their families went bankrupt."

(Mutsuo Utsunomiya, Oita prefecture)

"This year we are suffering from famine. By next yeas, will die of hunger or have no other choice but to kill ourselves. I have one of my sons in the Army. He is now in Manchuria. I wrote him the other day that he should be killed in battle. Then the government will give us compensation for his service and we will be able to survive this winter. Those who have daughters can sell them. I only have sons. But I think I can sell them that way."

(Excerpts from a report titled *"Take a walk in the starvation zone"* which was carried in the magazine *"Chuo Koron"* of February 1932)

Number of unemployed	
September 1929	268,590
September 1930	395,244
September 1931	425,526
September 1932	505,969

"I graduated from university, but ..."

Rate of employment among university and college graduates

1923　80 %　　1929　50 %　　1931　33 %

People Went to Manchuria Looking for "Arcadia"

A puppet regime was established in Manchukuo under the control of 600,000 Japanese troops

Settlers and their children who were sent to Manchuria pursuant to national policy.

Manchuria, showing Japanese settlements

Osaka Business Circles' attitude toward the Manchuria Incident

"The outbreak of Manchurian incident is nothing else but a self-defense act of our garrison against a provocative outrage of the Chinese Army. Nevertheless, the Chinese government appealed to the League of Nations for the resolution of the matter. It has ordered the people not to resist. But in reality, it instigated them to launch an anti-Japanese movement which runs counter to the international trust.

This is an overt hostile act against our country. We can never allow it. We have to secure our economic interests in Manchuria and demand that the Chinese government should prohibit immediately and strictly the anti-Japanese movement and assure no further resurgence."

The puppet regime robbed the local people of their land to provide Japanese settlers with farmland.

"The Japanese had bought a huge area of land in Manchuria – about 250,000 ha in total – even before the Manchurian Incident. The Chinese government and people accused Japan of plundering them of their land.

After the establishment of Manchukuo, the acquisition of land by the Japanese made rapid progress. That process was done to provide the Japanese settlers with farmland."

(Excerpts from the book *"The track of Japan in the modern times"*)

The Japanese Army blew up rail tracks in Manchuria and left equipment of the Chinese Army to frame the latter for the incident.

People Were Deprived of Their Freedom of Speech Because of the Intimidation by the Military Police, the Special Political Police and Attacks by the Media

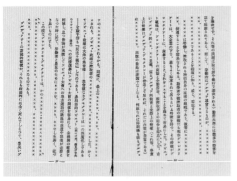

The censored words were represented by a series of Xs.

A poster calling for a total spiritual mobilization of the nation.

Children worshiped the sanctuary (imperial portrait) whenever they were on the way to and from school.

Organizations from trade unions to cultural groups were all suppressed

"The remaining forces in Shimonoseki city suffered a fatal blow in 1932. Organizations from trade unions, cultural groups to readers' circle were all suppressed."

(From the book *"Before and after prospects"* written by Masayoshi Fukuda)

No criticism of the war, the Emperor or the military was allowed

"At that time, not even a single word was allowed to be used against the war, the Emperor or the military. You could still criticize Hitler. But finally, the outbreak of the Japanese-Chinese War took away that remaining space."

(From the book *"Before and after prospects"* written by Masayoshi Fukuda)

People were looking for a breakthrough

"The censorship became more and more noticeable after the Manchurian Incident. Now it is difficult to find articles on current political, economic or social issues without censored words replaced by Xs.

All the people hate fascism. They want to cry out, but have no means. All anti-fascist voices are unorganized and looking for a breakthrough."

(From an article of *"Moji News"* written by Masayoshi Fukuda in November 1936)

Education was given strictly based on the Emperor-centered view of history

"Our country has the Emperor, a living god, and is the best country in the world. So it is proper that we possess Korea and Taiwan. It is the right of Japan as the leader of East Asia to conquer outrageous China and expand its occupying and ruling area. It is proper that we control the natives in the East. These were what we were taught through the education in family, school and society. As a result, militarist Japan sought hegemony, established a puppet state in Manchuria and became a target of criticism around the world."

(Taira Takahata, Tokyo)

Japan Began Full-scale Aggression on China under the Pretext of Punishing its Outrages

In Nanjing city, I saw so many bodies of massacred Chinese floating on the Yangtze River

"The Japanese-Chinese War broke out in 1937 immediately after I was called up for military service. I participated in an offensive operation in Nanjing city. Some say a massacre happened there. Others say it didn't happen. But I saw the reality with my eyes. When I approached Nanjing, I saw a mass of something black in the upper reaches of the Yangtze River. I thought there would be a mass of garbage. But they were dead bodies! I was outraged. I see that scene in my mind even now."

(Muneo Miyazaki, former navy man, Shimonoseki city)

Newspaper "Asahi Shinbun" carried articles in support of "our just war to punish China".

Why did Japan send its military troops to a foreign country and wage a war against it?

"I was recruited and joined the army in 1937 when I was 21 years old, just a few months before the outbreak of the war with China. The soldiers were miserable in the battlefield. One day, at the very moment when I said to a soldier next to me, 'Let's go!,' he stopped moving. A bullet had gone through his head. So many things happened in the battlefield that I cannot mention them all.

It was said that the war began because the Chinese Army shot first at the Japanese Army. But it was a war of aggression indeed. Why did Japan have to send its troops to a foreign country and wage war against it? That led to the war with the U.S."

(A disabled ex-soldier, Shimonoseki city)

Chinese prisoners of war were buried alive in Nanjing.

The Prime Minister Fumimaro Konoe

"The Empire has already reached to the limit of endurance. We could not avoid taking strong measures so we punished the atrocious Chinese armed forces and urged the Nanjing government to reflect on their acts, "

Japanese troops penetrated deeply into China.

Young People Were Forcibly Recruited as Soldiers through the Conscription System

Postage of a call-up paper costs only 1.5 sen

A scene at the physical examination for conscription. (1941)

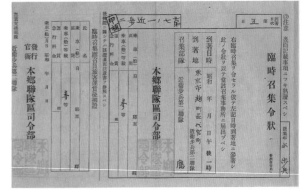

A call-up paper was called "red paper" because of its color.

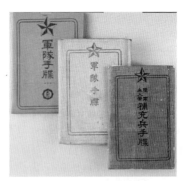

Soldiers' handbooks. The Imperial Rescript to Soldiers and Sailors and military regulations were printed.

Streamers used to see off the soldiers.

"I passed the physical examination for conscription in 1936 and was sent to the front line in China. Battle after battle for ten years. I was always thinking when I would be killed. That was my youth."

(Mutsuo Utsunomiya, Oita prefecture)

"My husband received a call-up paper and departed from the Moji port for Taiwan. I went to worship at a shrine many times and prayed that he would reach his destination safe and sound."

(Suwako Miyoshi, Shimonoseki city)

"Our price was only 1.5 sen (100 sen was equal to 1 yen), while a horse 800 yen. A soldier was treated worse than a horse."

(Hajime Kaneko, Shimonoseki city)

Japan Was Defeated by the Chinese People's War of Resistance
The more they advanced the more they were surrounded

A Chinese poster calling for anti-Japanese resistance and national salvation.

Japanese soldiers taking a nap after a "cleanup operation".

Japanese Army could occupy only points and lines and all around us seemed to be enemies

"An officer told us that we had occupied only a small part of the Chinese continent and all around us were enemies, so we could be shot anywhere, and gave each of us 30 bullets. I had my first battle in December 1941. We fought with the Eighth Route Army. I couldn't aim at the target. I was trembling and firing at random."

(Hisaichi Nagahara, Kitakyushu city)

The invading army couldn't win against the Chinese Eighth Route Army

"We couldn't win the war against the Eighth Route Army only by seizing important points. It was very difficult to keep them. We were superior in terms of the weapons. But we were beaten thoroughly. They destroyed rails between two points which we had seized. We ran out of food and ammunition and were stuck with no more supplies. It was said that Japan was defeated by the U.S. in the Pacific War. In fact, we had been beaten thoroughly in China. That was the decisive factor of the defeat of Japan."

(Mutsuo Utsunomiya, Oita prefecture)

Wounded soldiers were sent back from the battlefront. (September 1939)

The situation was the same as the present situation in Iraq

"I was wondering about the victory the U.S. declared after its seizure of Baghdad in this Iraqi war. It was the same as when the Japanese Army declared its victory after having seized only points and lines in China. That was as I thought. The U.S. established a puppet government. But it has no power. The U.S. and Japanese troops should withdraw from Iraq now."

(A former army soldier in his 90s, Shimonoseki city)

As of 1941, the main force of one million troops of the Japanese Army which had been mobilized for the war against China was stranded by the anti-Japanese war of resistance. In December 1941, when the Japan-U.S. war broke out, the war dead in China had exceeded 185,000. There was no prospect of Japan's winning the war.

The U.S. Participated in the War for the Purpose of Invading China and Occupying Japan

Not for the purpose of punishing Japan for its aggression and liberating Japan

A supply route which was used to transport U.S. aid materials to Chiang Kai-shek.

Gasoline was put under severe control in Japan because of its shortage caused by the U.S. sanctions.

War Plan Orange

"War Plan Orange" was a U.S. plan for war with Japan, which was drawn up after the Russo-Japanese War (1904-05). It was a long-range strategy for defeating and occupying Japan and seizing the Chinese market.

"The U.S. and Japan have been keeping their friendly relations, but someday a war will broke out between the two countries." "The root cause will be Japan's expansionist policy of aiming at controlling the land, men and resources in the Far East. The U.S. is a guardian of the western forces in this region." (1906)

"Japan will mobilize its total power for the war on which its national interests depend. When all preparations have been done, it will launch a surprise attack. Japan may be able to gain easily some targets in the West Pacific, but cannot expand its front line to the coast of the U.S. mainland. If Hawaii is attacked, our people will rise up in anger and endure the war for what they believe is just. Then we will begin an intensive counteroffensive, by taking advantage of our industrial power, regain the lost territories and command of the sea in the West Pacific, destroy Japan's military and economic power and drive it into unconditional surrender." (1906)

"Under the more difficult circumstances, the United States will fight by maritime strategy rather than intervention on the continent to remove Japan from Manchuria by U.S. alone. In so doing, the U.S. can exert maritime authority, restore lost ground, and will welcome the setting up of Japan's trade routes." "Extreme trade isolation in Japan drives it to ultimate poverty and exhaustion." "Unlimited war's reach is an unconditional victory." (1911)

"We will put under control all the waters surrounding Japan, enforce a blockade, isolate it by occupying all islands far from its mainland and put pressure by conducting air raids on its territory." (1923)

The U.S. took economic sanctions against Japan and waited for the latter's attack on Pearl Harbor

A year before the Pearl Harbor attack, U.S. Lieutenant Commander Arthur McCollum of the Office of Naval Intelligence submitted a memo to U.S. Navy Captains Walter Anderson and Dudley Knox.

"It is not believed that in the present state of political opinion the United States government is capable of declaring war against Japan without more ado. Therefore, the following course of action is suggested:

A. Make an arrangement with Britain for the use of British bases in the Pacific, particularly Singapore. B. Make an arrangement with Holland for the use of base facilities and acquisition of supplies in the Dutch East Indies. C. Give all possible aid to the Chinese government of Chiang-Kai-Shek. D. Send a division of long range heavy cruisers to the Orient, Philippines, or Singapore. E. Send two divisions of submarines to the Orient. F. Keep the main strength of the U.S. fleet now in the Pacific in the vicinity of the Hawaiian Islands. G. Insist that the Dutch refuse to grant Japanese demands for undue economic concessions, particularly oil. H. Completely embargo all U.S. trade with Japan, in collaboration with a similar embargo imposed by the British Empire.

Secret telegram and diary of U.S. Army Secretary Henry Stimson written 10 days prior to the "Pearl Harbor Attack"

"It is clear that diplomatic negotiations with Japan will be interrupted, and if Japan's strategic actions cannot be avoided, U.S. should initially not take obvious action at first." (Telegram)

"There is a risk for launching the first shot by Japan, but the U.S. should let Japan do it in order to get full support from our citizens. Whoever anyone sees, it is desirable to clarify so as not to hold any doubts who the invaders are."(Diary)

Japanese Rulers Rushed into War against the U.S. Even Though They Knew They Would Lose

Japan made an alliance with Germany and Italy and took the course of advancing to the south (1940)

"If the Japanese Army withdrew from China, that would mean its defeat. That would also reveal that the Imperial General Headquarters had deceived the people by announcing fake news on 'victories' and throw the country into great disorder. A revolution would result and the Emperor would be ousted. So the full withdrawal from China couldn't be accepted absolutely. Rather than that, the rulers rushed into war against the U.S. although they well knew that they would surely lose it."

(Mutsuo Utsunomiya, Oita prefecture)

Emperor's remarks

"We can do nothing unless we have any other alternative in dealing with the U.S. I am very anxious about the present situation. What will happen if Japan is defeated? If that becomes a reality, will the Prime Minister share all my burden?"

(From the "Diary of Kouichi Kido")

Commander of the combined fleet Isoroku Yamamoto's remarks

We will rampage for half a year or one year if we are ordered. But I am completely unsure whether we could fight for two or three years. I suggest that the utmost efforts be made to avoid the war against the U.S."

"To fight against the U.S. means to fight against almost the entire world. We cannot count on the Soviet Union. I will do my best and die in battle on board the battleship Nagato. But in the meantime, Tokyo will be burned down three times. I am sorry for Prime Minister Konoe. He will be torn apart by the people."

Navy Admiral Osami Nagano's remarks

"I have doubt whether we will win a victory over the enemy, needless to say, a great victory such as the victory in the Battle of the Japan Sea."

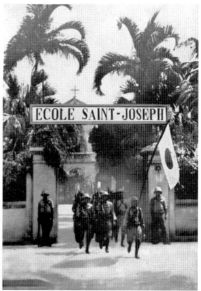

Japanese troops stationed in Hai Phong. (September 1940)

Japanese tanks in Nomenkan (May 1939). The Japanese Army was defeated decisively by the Soviet Army. That was a big factor in Japan's changing to the policy of advancing to the south.

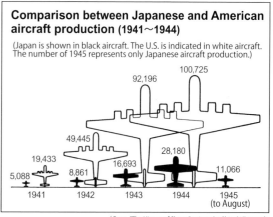

Comparison between Japanese and American aircraft production (1941〜1944)

(Japan is shown in black aircraft. The U.S. is indicated in white aircraft. The number of 1945 represents only Japanese aircraft production.)

	1941	1942	1943	1944	1945 (to August)
U.S.	19,433	49,445	92,196	100,725	
Japan	5,088	8,861	16,693	28,180	11,066

(From "The History of Showa" written by Shigeki Toyama)

Japan Occupied Southeast Asia as It Attacked Pearl Harbor

Burning U.S. warships in Pearl Harbor. (December 8, 1941)

People celebrating the falling of Singapore to the Japanese Army. (February 1942)

Battle of Midway. (June.1942)

U.S. Had Been Waiting for Japan to Attack It First

Japan won victories and occupied oil rich areas in the early stages of the war

"I was called up for military service in Shanghai on January 1, 1942. Japan occupied first such oil-rich areas as Borneo (Indonesia).

I participated in the battle off Surabaya, Indonesia. It was the first naval battle with the U.S., Britain and Holland and ended in a great victory for Japan. Until then, it was the best period for the Japanese Navy.

I participated in the battle of Midway. U.S. bases were on Midway Island, which was an important strategic point. But Japan's coded messages about the battle had been all deciphered by the U.S., which was waiting for the Japanese warships and destroyed them. The four aircraft carriers were sunk. The warplanes had no place to return to and all fell in the sea."

(Muneo Miyazaki, Shimonoseki city)

We were shocked to learn of our defeat in Midway

"The main force of my flying corps joined in the battle. We got the news that our forces were fatally beaten. We were shocked to learn that the news was true."

(Isao Maeda, Shimonoseki city)

Japanese warships were sunk by U.S. submarines because Japan's code had already been deciphered

"I joined the Navy in 1943. Our first mission was to escort a medicine-carrying ship to Saipan Island. But the ship was attacked and sunk by the U.S. submarines. The Japan's code was already all deciphered by the U.S."

(Katsumi Saruwatari, Shimonoseki city)

Japan's Retreat from Guadalcanal Island a Year and Half after the Outbreak of the War Marked a Turning Point in the War

Citizens of Sapporo in a ceremony for receiving the ashes of those who died an "honorable death" on Attu Island. (October 1942)

Only a single contingent was dispatched to retake the airfield in Guadalcanal. As a result, all soldiers were killed. (January 1943)

Both Army and Navy suffered a succession of miserable defeats

"I participated in the battle on Guadalcanal Island. It was a cruel battle. About 10,000 army soldiers died of hunger. It was just like hell on earth. Both Army and Navy suffered defeat after defeat. Two vessels on which I was on board were sunk by the U.S. When I experienced the first sinking, we were going to help the army which had suffered a crushing blow. But our vessel was hit by some torpedoes. I was rescued by a Japanese submarine, but many died. Some were killed by the crews of their own vessel. Some others were eaten by sharks. Only 13 people out of 250 were saved."(Muneo Miyazaki, Shimonoseki city)

"The Navy knew that it could only fight for one year. That was true. We won victories in the first year. Later, the four aircraft carriers were sunk in the South Pacific. Everybody knew that going to the battlefront meant death. Nevertheless, we couldn't help seeing off our comrades in arms."(A war survivor in his 80s, Shimonoseki city)

Reinforcements disembarked on the island at night to form a force 6,000 strong. Out of them, however, 1,500 were lost.

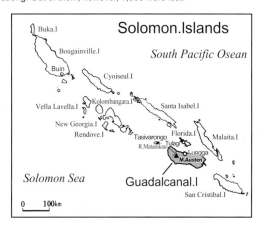

Tojo Government Collapsed After Saipan Island Fell to U.S. But Japan Still didn't Stop the War

Japanese garrisons in Saipan were all destroyed.(1944)

A poster of the 38th anniversary of the Japanese Army reads "Shoot without ceasing."

"It was said that Japan was still winning. But I was very surprised to see the soldiers going to the front with bamboo (not metal) canteens. At that time, I thought Japan would lose the war. Why didn't the Japanese government stop the war when Saipan Island had fallen to the enemy and many soldiers were dying an "honorable death" in various places?"

(A disabled ex-soldier, Shimonoseki city)

"When the Tojo government resigned in September 1934, there was a rumor that probably the war would end soon. A Chinese merchant who I had a talk with in Sumatra was also saying so. I think the ruling people must also have known something."

(Hisao Komatsu, Shimonoseki city)

U.S. had command of the sea and air

"The command of the sea and air was totally in enemy hands. It was merely a dream to go back to Japan. I was in the Truk Islands. One day, a soldier was suspected of having stolen a watch from an officer. He was beaten to death. But it was written in his official record that he died from malaria. We must not forget that there were such horrible stories that we couldn't mention, even among the stories of those who died and were praised for their courage."

(Isao Maeda, Shimonoseki city)

"I stayed in Rabaul for seven months. We had U.S. air raids so often. U.S. warplanes even bombed our hospital several times although we had put a huge Red Cross sign on the roof. Many soldiers suffered from malaria and dengue fever. The sanitary conditions were very bad, so you could find bedbugs and lice everywhere. Most of the hospitalized patients were suffering from skin diseases. Some had come from New Guinea, suffering from malnutrition. A number of wounded soldiers were brought in sometimes from New Guinea in the middle of the night. Most of them were found dead the next morning. I was thinking that Japan will lose the war soon."

(Emiko Okada, former war nurse, Osaka prefecture)

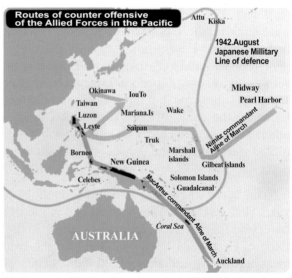

(This data comes from "The History of Showa;the seventh volume" Published by Kenshu shuppan)

Tragedies in the Naval Battle of Leyte and Battlefronts in the Philippines

We were in no condition to fight as we had no supplies

"I joined in the naval battle of Leyte (Philippines) as a medic. Our warship was sunk by the U.S. Navy. I was rescued and brought to Cavite by the local people. My original unit ordered me not to go back to Japan, but to be deployed to an airfield there. I went to that airfield. There were no pilots there because all had been killed in the suicide attacks. I found only maintenance men.

In January 1945, ground units of the Navy were formed to defend Manila. But most of the soldiers had not been given fighting training. Two battalions were annihilated by the U.S. air raids. I escaped from Manila. It was the start of our escape journey which continued for half a year. We stayed in the mountains, looking for something to eat. We had no supplies like ammunition and food. If we shot one bullet, the enemy responded with tens of bullets. We were in no condition to fight battles."

(Tomikichi Sakai, Nagasaki city)

Japanese soldiers killed in a battle in Ormoc. (Leyte Island)

Wounded soldiers. (Luzon Island)

Soldiers died of malnutrition

"In Baguio (Luzon Island), the patients died of malnutrition one after another, We were given a little rice. Probably they were not given rice at all. The dead bodies were thrown into a big hole in the ground. I felt pity for them.

I thought how their relatives would feel if they knew that the soldiers were not killed in battle but died of hunger. There were no ashes of the dead soldiers. We put their hair and nails in white wooden boxes and send them to Japan."

(Emiko Okada, former war nurse, Osaka prefecture)

War nurses in Rabaul (Papua New Guinea).
A group of them were sent later to Mindanao Island,
Philippines and all died there from malnutrition or by their own hands.

Dead Bodies of Soldiers Were Scattered They Died of Hunger or Killed Themselves in the Burma - Imphal Operation

The 18th Division of the Japanese Army was annihilated in Hukawng (Myanmar).

In the Imphal Operation, soldiers crossed 2,500m high mountains covered with a 50km wide expanse of dense woodland.

Soldiers killed themselves by grenades because they had no supply of food and ammunition

"I participated in the Imphal Operation. The Japanese troops burned local villages which they didn't need to burn and killed local civilians who they didn't need to kill. Many of us also died one after another. More died of malaria, amoebic dysentery and malnutrition than in battle. It was because food and ammunition were not supplied after the enemy bombed roads and bridges to cut the transportation routes.

First, soldiers killed themselves one by one, using a grenade for each person. Later, when they ran short of grenades, they committed mass suicide, using a grenade for a group. When the grenades ran out, an injection of poison was given to those who couldn't move due to malaria. They couldn't set foot on Japanese soil again. Out of 4,000 soldiers of our regiment, only 300 survived and came back to Japan alive." (Niichi Kuba, Shimonoseki city)

I cut a little finger off my dead comrade in arms and brought it back home

"It was only in May 1945 when we began to retreat at last. We walked 1,200km in 140 days with bare feet in the rain, suffering from hunger and diseases. If you couldn't keep up with your unit, you would be given a grenade. Those soldiers who couldn't follow their comrades fell down one after another. I cut a little finger off my comrade in arms who died after he got stuck in the mud and couldn't pull out himself.

When we crossed the Sittoung River, half of our troops were carried away and tens of thousands of dead bodies were piled up in the lower reaches of the river. Black vultures were flocking on the dead. I passed scattered bodies of some soldiers killed by the mines. Among them, I saw a dead body without legs (blown away by the mine) standing as Dharma and swarming with flies. I also saw a dead body lying on his back with a rice plant growing in his mouth." (Atsumi Oda, Okayama prefecture)

Many Soldiers Deserted or Died from Diseases on Chinese Battlefronts

Preparations for transporting wounded soldiers after an operation.

Soldiers marching with "white wooden boxes" (containing ashes of their comrades in arms) in front of their chest. (1942)

Many soldiers dropped out in the march because of fatigue and heat. A soldier taking care of his comrade in arms who lagged behind.

I experienced a 1,200km long forced march along the Yangtze River

"I joined the army in December 1944. I was deployed to a front line near Nanking in China after one week training. One day when I was sent to a flying corps of the Army to do some work, I saw only fake warplanes. There was no Hayabusa (falcon) famous fighter planes. We were running short of food so that we couldn't eat our fill. There were some soldiers looking for leftover food.

One month later, we were ordered to join the march along the Yangtze River. We marched in the snow and rain during the night to avoid air raids. It was very hard for new conscripts like me. To fall behind in the march meant death. We had lost 30 percent of our troops when we reached the destination.

After the 1200km long march, we battled against the Eighth Route Army. We had fierce battles day after day. Many were killed and wounded. After every battle we transported the wounded in the dawn, gathered the dead and burned them. That was a routine which made us feel so bad.

Our company consisted of only 40 soldiers (rather than the typical 90). Of these, about ten were experienced soldiers - the others were new conscripts. We had only one machine gun (usually three for a company). We had only old-type rifles." (Hiroitsu Kawano, Shimonoseki city)

Our priority was to find food over and above fighting battles

"Into 1945, the more battles we fought the more losses we suffered. The supplies didn't reach us. New recruits were brought in sometimes, but we were short of food and ammunition. We had to fight with our bayonets as weapons and find food by ourselves. In the last stages of the war, our priority was to find food over and above fighting battles." (Hisaichi Nagahara, Kitakyushu city)

Imperial Headquarters Intentionally Carried Out such Operations That Would Kill more Soldiers

Kurita Fleet's U-turn caused unnecessary sacrifices

"In the naval battle of Leyte, Japan had an operation plan to draw the attention of the U.S. fleet by using four aircraft carriers and some escort warships as decoys, for the purpose of getting the Japanese combined fleet under the command of Vice Admiral Kurita in the Leyte Gulf.

I was on board the Chitose, one of the decoys. The four carriers had no warplanes. They were all sunk as a natural result of the U.S. attack. Most of the crew members were killed. Strangely enough, however, the combined fleet didn't get into the bay, but made a U-turn. The decoys including the crew were destroyed and killed for nothing. It was the height of absurdity. Was the U-turn a directive from the headquarters? Or, was Kurita so frightened? He didn't talk about that until he died. The truth is still veiled."

(Tomikichi Sakai, Nagasaki city)

A Japanese destroyer exploding due to U.S. bombers' attack. (off Leyte)

Soldiers listening to their senior officer's address before rushing on the enemy with drawn swords.

The Imperial General Headquarters announced that all soldiers had died although the fighting was still going on

"The enemy forces began landing on Saipan Island on June 15, 1945. Fierce battles broke out on the ground. We received on July 7 a radio announcement of the Imperial General Headquarters that all our forces had charged the enemy's positions and died an honorable death. But our forces were still resisting in various places – mountains, valleys, jungles. We saw them from Tinian Island. Out of 45,000 troops, more than 10,000 were still alive. The Imperial General Headquarters' announcement was a deceptive maneuver to take the minds of the people off Saipan by describing as if all had been already killed. This was because it had no relief force to dispatch and was afraid that the people would get angry to know that it was not thinking of any relief action.

The media which reported death for honor of the Saipan garrison..

The Imperial General Headquarters did nothing but drove so many young soldiers who had already lost their fighting power to die what they call on honorable death."

(Kenji Yasuoka, Shimonoseki city)

The suicide attack squad Shiragiku was formed only to urge soldiers into killing themselves

"I knew for the first time only when I came back home that suicide attack squads had been formed and I had lost many of my friends who had joined them. In the last months of the war, the suicide attack squad Shiragiku (white chrysanthemum) had been formed with training planes only to urge soldiers into killing themselves. I cannot help crying always when I consider the feelings of my comrades in arms who must have worried but rushed into the enemy resolutely in the end."

(Kenji Yasuoka, Shimonoseki city)

Comrades in arms seeing off a suicide fighter.

Even Family Men in Their 40s were Recruited as Soldiers

I thought that I wouldn't be called up for the time being

"I passed the physical examination for conscription in July 1940. I was categorized into the second class. It was said that those in the second class would be recruited only in case of emergency. So I thought that I wouldn't be called up for the time being.

But one day in May 1941, when I was working at a workshop, I was asked to present myself at the company office. There I was given a "red paper" (call-up paper), which could decide on the human life by 1.5 cent postage." (Hisaichi Nagahara, Kitakyushu city)

A soldier having a pleasant chat with his family during visiting hours in a barracks yard.

"My father was 40 years old when he was taken from our family for the military service. He had a poor physique and had failed to pass the examination for conscription. We were thinking that he wouldn't be called up. But he was recruited as reservist and sent to the south. He got malaria there and died three days after he came home." (A man in his 60s, Shimonoseki city)

New recruits in their 30s or 40s aroused our deepest compassion

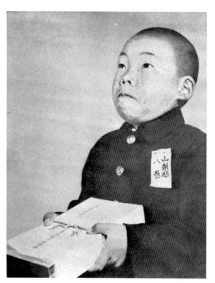

"I felt sorry for the new (but far older than we) recruits in their 30s or 40s. They didn't have a good physique. They were married and had children. They were deployed to the front line like Saipan and Tinian although they had been trained only for six months. Such people like those who were still standing when they were ordered 'Lie down!' to hide themselves from the enemy's attack were killed first." (Kenji Yasuoka, Shimonoseki city)

A war orphan who has lost his father in the battlefront.

I was wounded and discharged from the army, but I was called up again

"I was wounded in Shanghai and was sent to a hospital in Japan. I was discharged from the army and got a job in the National Railways. But I was called up again in March 1945. Usually, a man like me would be exempted from military service. Japan was in such a very difficult situation that anybody could be recruited. I got training to destroy enemy's tanks by putting mines in front of them. It was too hard for older or disabled men. It was obvious that Japan would be defeated." (A man at the age of 88, Shimonoseki city)

"At that time, any man, however he might be - one-eyed or feeble - was recruited." (Yoshiko Tajima, Shimonoseki city)

U.S. Forces Were Cruel and Conducted Exterminatory Operations

U.S. used flame throwers against Japanese troops hiding in caves in the battle of Iwo Island.

Japanese hospital ship "Buenos Aires" sinking after the bombing attack by the Allied Forces in the South Pacific.

Americans machine-gunned our soldiers swimming in the sea after their vessel had been sunk

"The Japanese forces were completely defeated in the naval battle of Guadalcanal. The U.S. forces machine-gunned and killed Japanese soldiers drifting in the sea. The Japanese Navy rescued the Russian sailors of the Baltic Fleet in the Battle of the Japan Sea during the Russo-Japanese War, while the U.S. forces massacred even unarmed people." (A former navy man, Shimonoseki city)

The same thing happened when the battleship Yamato was sunk

"When the battleship Yamato was sunk, I was wounded in the head and left shoulder. I saw a number of soldiers swimming and calling for help. I was shocked to see a U.S. warplane machine-gunning and killing them one by one. I didn't believe that a human being could do such a cruel thing.

I was rescued by a Japanese destroyer. I was treated at a naval hospital and was transferred to Kure, Hiroshima prefecture. I saw from there the mushroom cloud of the atomic bomb in Hiroshima. The U.S. has perpetrated the cruelest acts against Japan. Why does it say that Japan committed the worst crimes when it saved Japan?"
(Hiroshi Konishi, former crew member of Yamato, Shimonoseki city)

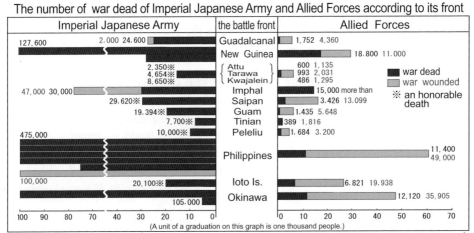

The number of war dead of Imperial Japanese Army and Allied Forces according to its front

(A unit of a graduation on this graph is one thousand people.)
(This data comes from "The History of Showa ; the eighth volume" published by Kenshushuppan.)

Japanese Soldiers Were Put on Board Troopships without Firearms or Food and Sent Abroad to Be Killed

Many Japanese ships were sunk by U.S. submarines in the Bashi Channel

"I was in Manchuria until 1943, when I came home. But I was recruited again in July 1944. We were heading for the Philippines. On September 9, when we were passing the Bashi Channel, our troopship was hit by three torpedos. Our ship had a displacement of 3,500 tons. But it sank in only five minutes. I was sitting on the deck when the ship was attacked. I was blown away into the sea and drifted hanging on to a piece of wood. There were many dead bodies floating on the sea. I was rescued after eight hours by a Japanese warship. Only a small number, maybe one fifth, were saved. So many were killed."

(A man at the age of 82, Shimonoseki city)

Japanese people drifting in the sea after having escaped from a sinking vessel off the Palau Islands.

A Japanese troopship in a desperate effort to escape from U.S. attack.

We were given wooden guns and bamboo knives

"I departed from Fukuoka for Pusan, south Korea, by troopship in the night of January 4, 1945. We were given weapons before our departure. But a real rifle was given to only one in five soldiers. The rest were given wooden 'rifles.' Knives were made of bamboo. We didn't have enough training. We were put on a train and moved only at night to avoid the air raids by B29 bombers."

(Hajime Kaneko, Shimonoseki city)

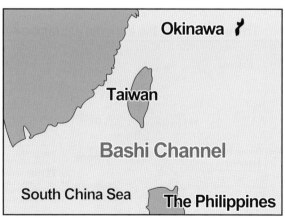

Bashi Channel

It Was Not an Ordinary War
No Food Reached Us

Departure of Japanese students for the battlefront.

A Japanese soldier drinking water from a canteen of his wounded comrade in arms.

"I was called up for military service in the winter of 1943 and was sent to a southern island. So many schoolmates of mine were killed. The sea swallowed up 3,000 soldiers in an instant together with their ship. The forced fatigues killed one after another those people who didn't have to be have died. It didn't take so much time for 300 soldiers to be reduced to 30. Soldiers died in the jungle, saying, "I don't want to die" "I want to eat rice with a rice bowl" "I want to go home, go home, go back to Japan." Soldiers from Okinawa went crazy when they heard the sad news about their island. Some deserted. But they were captured and shot to death by their own comrades in arms under orders from their officer. After a succession of indiscriminate bombings and machine - gunnings, a surprise attack team was formed. They gave a feeble shout of encouragement from their empty stomach and rushed on the enemy only with swords. When our comrades in arms died, we didn't cremate their entire bodies. The cremated part changed from an arm to a forearm, from a wrist to a finger. When we went to a field hospital to receive the dead body of our comrade in arms, a doctor carelessly cut a wrist off his body, wrapped it, put it in his mess kit and gave it to us silently. There are more stories. Innumerable stories are still within my hateful memory."

(Excerpts from *"Judgement in August"* written by Hideo Isonaga)

I ate lizards and snakes to survive

"In October 1944, I was in New Guinea. All food-transporting vessels were attacked and sunk by the U.S. Nothing reached us. We were eating even trunks of papaya and banana trees, lizards, snakes, frogs, etc. to survive. Many fellow soldiers died of hunger.

I myself suffered from malaria and beriberi. I couldn't walk. I thought that I would surely die unless I ate something. I crawled on my hands and knees to the shore and ate seaweed. I should have died if I had been rescued one week later. The company I belonged to consisted of about 300 soldiers at first. But so many were killed that we have not been able to have a reunion of our company."

(Katsumi Saruwatari, Shimonoseki city)

The war dead of the Imperial Japanese Army according to area of the Pacific War

Number of deaths
- This mark shows one hundred thousand people.
- This mark represents ten thousand people.

Soviet Union mainland 52,700
Mongolia 1,700
Manchuria 245,400
the Chinese mainland 467,500
the north of Korea 34,600
the south of Korea 18,900
Aleutian Kuril Is. Sakhalin 24,400
Ioto Is. 20,100
Burma, India 167,000
Taiwan 41,900
Okinawa Is. 186,500
the Central Pacific Islands 249,000
  Guam 21,000
  Saipan 55,300
  Tinian 15,500
  Angaur 1,200
  Peleliu 10,100
  Woleai Is. 5,000
  Truk Is. 8,400
  Marshall Is. 19,200
  Gilbert 5,500
  the rest of islands 106,700
Philippines Is. 518,000
French Indochina 12,400
Thailand Malaysia Singapore 21,000
Java, Sumatra Celebes 25,400
the war dead sank in the sea on the way to the front 103,000
the South Pacific Islands 346,900
  the West New Guinea 82,600
  Lesser Sunda Is.
  Borneo 18,000
  the East New Guinea 127,600
  Solomon Is. 88,200
  Bismarck Arch. 30,500

Notes
①The number of deaths shows the total, including soldiers and army civilian employees belonging to the army and the navy, those who were killed, wounded, diseased and disappeared in battle. It also includes 188,000 people who died in the war between Japan and China.
②The correct number of the wounded and diseased person in the war is unclear.
③An estimated number of crippled persons reaches 83,000 in the army and 13,000 in the navy. (There is other estimated number of disabled persons that amounts to 53,000 in the army and 8,000 in the navy.)
④An approximate number of the war dead according to armed forces is estimated to be about 1,900,000 in the army and about 630,000 in the navy.

(This data comes from "The History of Showa ; the seventh volume" published by Kenshushuppan.)

Many Died of Diseases or Hunger

Unboiled water caused amoebic dysentery

In the spring of the last year of WWII, lots of Japanese soldiers were sent to guard Manchuria in crisis. Many of them belonged to my division which was stationed at Konan Province. Each of them was forced to walk all the way to Manchuria from Konan, shouldering a gun. Of course, they quenched their thirst with unboiled water along the wayside. Naturally quite a few of them contracted amoebic dysentery and had loose bowels during the hard march. Most of them wasted away and lost their lives. (Setsuo Ikeda from Shimonoseki city)

A Japanese soldier's dead body in Guadalcanal Island, island of hunger. (1943)

Many soldiers died of malaria

In 1943, it was evident that Japan would be defeated. I was dispatched from South China to Osaka, Japan to lead a party of recruits, but there was no convoy ship and no petroleum. In addition, many troopships toward South China could not arrive at the destination. Most of these were attacked by U.S. Navy and were sunk on the way. (A man in his eighties)

Japanese soldier's gathering banana buds to stave off their hunger during the Imphal Operation. (1944)

Soldiers in Rabaul clearing forest land for cultivation to feed themselves.

It Was U.S. Forces that Burned Down Manila and Chinese City of Changsha

U.S. forces burned down the city and burned citizens to death

"The U.S. forces burned down Manila with warplanes, mortars, howitzers and tanks. When they found buildings where Japanese soldiers might be hidden, they destroyed them one by one. We had only three old-type cannons, some rifles which had been used during the Russo-Japanese War and bamboo spears, while the U.S. army had automatic rifles. We were hiding as much as we could rather than fighting against the enemy. The commander of the Japanese garrison committed suicide on February 26. Two battalions (800~1,000 troops) were annihilated. It has been said that the Japanese army burned down the city of Manila and massacred the citizens. But the Japanese army had no spare power to do this. It was the U.S. forces that massacred the citizens by indiscriminate bombings." (Tomikichi Sakai, Nagasaki city)

They made indiscriminate air raids in China too

"My unit was stationed in Changsha. One night, B29 bombers raided this city of 250,000 people that was as large as Shimonoseki city. The U.S. burned down the city in one night. Local residents told me that Changsha was not the only city which has been raided by the U.S." (Setsuo Ikeda, Shimonoseki city)

City of Manila burned to the ground by U.S. air raids and bombardment.

A Chinese city under air raid by U.S. bombers B29 that served also as a trial of air raid on Japan with incendiary bombs.

A U.S. B25 bomber attacking a bridge on the Yellow River in China.

U.S. warplanes targeted hospitals with Red Cross signs

"U.S. warplanes began to fly over our heads around 1943 when the Japanese army got exhausted. We didn't move by day and cooked meals by night. The following day, the U.S. made an indiscriminate bombing in those areas where they noticed the smoke. The U.S. burned down cities and towns indiscriminately under the pretext that there must be Japanese soldiers there. It is the same way as the U.S. used also in Afghanistan where they bombed the country by saying that Bin Laden must be there. The U.S. also bombed field hospitals in China. The international law prohibits the attacking of facilities with Red Cross signs. After the war, the U.S. glossed over its crimes by insisting that those happened mistakenly and not on purpose. This is also the same way as they have used in Iraq. It is an outrageous argument that the air raids on all cities and atomic bombings can be justified in revenge of Pearl Harbor. But this is the U.S.!"

(Hisaichi Nagahara, Kitakyushu city)

"We Won't Want Anything Until We Win the War."

People couldn't speak out in the home front

Students were forced to work in munitions factories

"The Wartime Education Exemption Law was enforced in 1945 to make high-school students graduate earlier and recruit them for the military. The students graduated after having finished their fourth grade although the high schools had five grades. The students already in the fifth grade received red papers (call-up papers), while those in the fourth grade received pink papers (stand-by papers) and were told to stand by at home."

(Kaoru Inoue, Shimonoseki city)

Schoolgirls serving as labor force.

"The high-school students in the first and second grades worked in the countryside. They buried drains or did farm work. The third-grade students went to a factory of the Kobe Steel Company to produce pipes and plates for airplanes. Students were coming also from other high schools including female high schools. All worked very hard. We were given plain food as lunch but no wages."

(Jiro Masumoto, Shimonoseki city)

We couldn't speak out freely

"I was in the fourth grade of the elementary school when my teacher told us at a morning classroom meeting, 'If you find strange people walking around Hinoyama, they must be spies gathering information about the military fortress. Don't answer when such strange people ask you about the roads and places. Don't go with them even if they give you candies. When you come across such strange people, tell me as soon as possible.'"

(Susumu Tokumura, Shimonoseki city)

A signboard calling for spiritual mobilization of the whole nation.

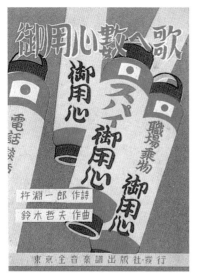
The text of a song arousing vigilance against spies.

"During the war, some agents of the Special Political Police were inside the factories of the Kobe Steel Company. No one could speak out against the war."

(Eiji Yamamoto, Shimonoseki city)

Food Shortages during the War

Rice and Sugar Rationed

Requisitioning of Rice in Shimonoseki. (1945)

Ration Tickets

"War broke out when I was in the 4th grade, and for the next five years I grew up in the midst of war. I didn't receive a proper education because I had to work in potato fields or was assigned military duties. Not enough food, no strength, no education at home. People used to say that you shouldn't marry a woman who grew up in this era. With the food shortages, rice and sugar were rationed. We also needed a ticket for clothing." (Owner, Fujinaga Clothing Store, Hikoshima)

"During the war, there was not enough food or other necessities. When I was in elementary school, we were told to hand in aluminum lunch boxes as building material for airplanes. We collected oil from pine trees and other plants in the mountain. Our school ground was turned into a field to grow sweet potatoes and pumpkins. We planted soybeans and sweet potatoes even on the banks of a little river by the airfield." (Toshie Shimada, Oki)

Clothing Tickets

"As a child, I grew up under the national slogans 'Americans and British, Evil Beasts; We Desire Nothing Until Victory; Fire and Never Quit!' When I was in the 5th and 6th grade, we worked hard to increase food production. Later, we were sent from school to help in the nearby farm. We were given a slice of sweet potato as a snack, and I remember how delicious it was. It angers me to see kids on TV nowadays who waste or play with food." (Susumu Tokumura, Yamanokuchi-cho)

"At the height of the war in 1944, I was married dressed in work pants. The ceremony was simple. We exchanged ceremonial drinks witnessed by our parents and siblings. We couldn't afford to have a wedding ceremony. We hardly had enough food to survive." (Miyoko Nawa, Hikoshima)

"Listen to the Voices from the Sea"

Writings of Fallen Student Soldiers in World War Ⅱ (Extract)

"Note of Japanese students killed in war" afterword 1949 (abstract)

Hideo Odagiri

Though the war was over, and only four years has passed, a suspicious smell of war begins to drift again. What will happen to the Japanese? We cannot afford to just watch this development in silence. The people who had deep sorrow gathered and have begun to stand up hand in hand to keep peace and freedom. How else can we act ? Meetings of the peaceful protection were organized at Tokyo, Osaka and other cities, agreed with peace protection world meeting of Paris. "An association of the intellectual" was organized. Labor unions and progress political parties, cultural organizations have given declarations of peace and have talked about strong determinations. This book is published in such a situation. This record, left with a large quantity of blood recklessly lost will press the heart of all people reading this for deep wisdom, consideration and determination for such blood to not be lost again.

The last letter to his mother
Ichizo Hayashi

From Fukuoka High School, entered Kyoto Imperial University, Faculty of Economics.
Killed in action as a member of Special Attack Unit, April 12, 1945, off Okinawa.
He was twenty-three years old.

My dear Mother: The time has finally come for me to write a very sad letter.

How will the parents' loving hearts, even exceeding the love of a child for its parents, hear of the news of today?

[The last farewell poem of Shoin Yoshida, 1830-59]

I think of this poem because it touches my heart so very deeply.

I have been truly blessed with so much happiness. I know did all sorts of self-centered things, didn't I?

But please forgive me and attribute all that selfish behavior to my immature over-dependence on you.

I am pleased to have the honor of having been chosen as a member of a Special Attack Force that is on its way into battle, but I cannot help crying when I think of you, Mom.

When I reflect on the hopes you had for my future, Mom, and how you brought me up as though it were a matter of life and death, I feel so sad that I am going to die without doing anything to bring you joys or to relieve your worries.

I may not be a great person, but I still cannot ever say to you:

"Mom, please give me up," or "Please be happy that I died honorably." But please do not let me say too much about this sort of thing; after all, you always know exactly what I am thinking anyway.

Students marching on the street after having participated in a sendoff ceremony.

A Chinese civilian full of blood
Tadashi Kawashima

Through the Preparatory Division, he entered Tokyo University of Agriculture,
in 1937 and graduated in 1940. Conscripted and entered the barracks,
December 1 1940, and transferred to the Northern China Garrison, China.
Died on January 3, 1945. Army lieutenant.
He was twenty-nine years old.

January 31,1943 Clear

At 1:30 in the middle of the night, headquarters called to send us on a punitive expedition at 5:30 a.m.-A hike in the cold and dark on what remains of the snow.

One soldier from Nakazawa Company hit a Chinese civilian with a rock. Full of blood and with his skull smashed, the man fell to the ground. The soldier kicked him as he lay there, and then used another stone. I could not stand watching that. But the officers of Nakazawa company were there too, taking it all in coldly and without emotion. Apparently it had all been done by order of sub-lieutenant Takagi.

A particularly heartless man! When I think about what happened to that innocent man I ask myself why I did not try to come to his aid, even though it would have been too late and a useless effort. When I think like that, a wave of self-reproach hits me. A woman who must have been his wife was weeping as she held on tightly to the bleeding man. But he didn't die! In fact, as soon as the troop moved off, he got up and, supported by his wife, hobbled away very slowly.

I would never, ever, allow any child of mine to be a soldier -anything but a soldier!… Peace! World peace is the very highest priority.

U.S. Air Raids on Japanese Cities

Testimonies gathered in various places
by the National Campaign Caravan for
the Atomic Bomb Exhibition

After the outbreak of the Japan - U.S. War in 1941,
Japan was beaten in the naval battle of Midway the
next year and in the battle of Guadalcanal one and a
half years later. In June 1944, Saipan Island called
"invincible fortress" and Tinian Island fell to the U.S.,
which seized command of the air and sea in the Pacific
and were able to attack Japan's mainland from the air.

Japan's defeat was an undeniable fact. In July 1944,
the Tojo cabinet collapsed. But the Japanese government
based on the Emperor system didn't end its reckless war.
Moreover, it sent troopships without escort warships and
let them be sunk one after another by the U.S. Navy. In
the southern islands, many soldiers who were left behind
died of hunger and disease. The war dead increased
drastically in 1944.

The U.S. began to make air raids on the Japanese
mainland. The first large-scale air raid was the Tokyo
air raid on March 10, 1945, which was followed by
other cities like Osaka, Nagoya and so on. The U.S.
forces carried out indiscriminate air raids to burn a
total of 67 cities the ground and massacre hundreds
of thousands of people.

The point of this map shows the place
that received U.S. air raids.

Devastation of Great Tokyo Air Raid on March 10, 1945
—Why did they have to kill 100,000 people?—

Charred bodied lying on the roadside after Tokyo Air Raid. (Asakusa Hanakawado)

American B-29s fire-bombed Asakusa, Honjo, Fukagawa, and Edogawa cities on both sides of the Sumida River to build a ring of fire, trapping the citizens into the center. Then they showered 1783 tons of fire bombs onto them.

"I thought I felt a drop of rain, but it was gasoline. In an instant we were in a sea of flames."

"People were burned to death in Sumida River since the oil on the river surface was burning."

"People were looking for family members in the floating bodies on the Sumida River. They retrieved and cremated them back at the shelters. Among the dead were mostly women and children. I will never forget their sinful act, knowing the end of the war was near."

Homeless people carrying furniture and belongings, seeking relatives or friends.

People retrieving the bodies from the river after the U.S. air-raid on Tokyo. (Near Kikukawa-bashi Bridge, Honjo)

Only the Imperial Palace was not attacked?

There is no monument commemorating the Tokyo Air Raid. Seen in the photo is the Kannon (Bodhisattva of compassion) temple by the Meiji-za Theatre site.

Many people took shelter in Meiji-za Theatre since they thought it was built of steel frames and safe inside. However, it was a wooden building and completely burnt down. At the gate was a pile of dead bodies still burning until the next morning. For the next three days, people couldn't even open their eyes because of the pain caused by the smoke and foul smell.

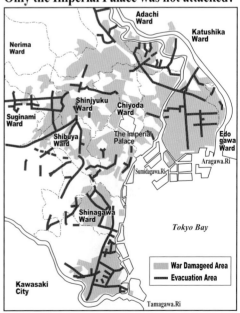

30

All Died, Limbs Ripped Apart

Nagoya Air Raid
March 12th, 19th, 25th

"In March of 1945 I was caught in the air raids of Nagoya. I was in the 4th grade. I had just come back home to my parents from the place I was evacuated to because there was not enough food at the evacuation site. We were all surrounded by fire, some neighbors who had left the shelters were all found dead, with limbs torn off, the next morning."

"Even after the air raids on Nagoya and Ichinomiya, Americans fired machine guns to kill everyone they could find, but they didn't destroy the railways or train stations."

Looking over Nagoya Port from the rooftop of Matsuzaka-ya Department Store.

Osaka Air Raid
March 13 (Midnight) — 14

"I was a 4th grader when Nishi-Yodogawa was bombed. After running away from the fire I found myself in Umeda from where I could see the faraway Takashimaya Department Store because the whole city was completely leveled to the ground. Under the bridge there were piles and piles of dead bodies, it was a horrible sight."

"Numerous bombs were dropped on Kyobashi Station and its surrounding

People desperately fighting the fires. (Kita-ku Ward, Osaka)

area, killing 500 people all at once. People couldn't bear the heat from the bombing, found no place to escape but to jump into the boiling water of the river where they died. I still can't forget the horror. U.S. fighters killed with machine guns everyone they found in the rice fields. My father was killed at the age of 43."

Kobe Air Raid
March 17th, May 11th, & June 5th

"Fire bombs destroyed the whole area near Motomachi Station."

People evacuating after the air-raid. (Kobe)

Pumping water to extinguish fires.

Bombing to Surround Cities
June: Air Attacks of Rural Cities Begin

Completely destroyed Kagoshima City.

Kagoshima Air Raid — June 17

"Kagoshima city was completely burned to the ground after the air raid. Chiran was also bombed because of its airfield."

Hamamatsu City in flames after air raids.

Hamamatsu Air Raid — June 18

"Dead people were all over. This area was a railway hub, and all of the tracks were destroyed. American fleets were approximately 40 km off the shore of Enshu-nada, and bombarded the city from there. I saw beached torpedo duds all over. Americans used napalm to incinerate the entire non-residential area, killing civilians senselessly."

Devastation of Yokkaichi City. City hall is seen on left.

Yokkaichi Air Raid — June 18

"On June 18, 1945, a 2 km² area around the city building was totally burned down during the early morning hours. More than 800 civilians were killed in one night. A fire bomb hit our house while we were still asleep, and my father and I, still in pajamas, managed to escape. Suddenly, the roof collapsed and the whole house was ablaze, with my mother and younger brother trapped inside. I dashed inside with my father and rescued my mother and brother, but they were severely burnt and did not survive. We could not have a funeral for them because we didn't have enough money. When we took their bodies to the crematory, I remember seeing piles of coffins.

B-29 dropping fire bombs.

Cities were Burnt to Ashes Every Night

Shizuoka Air Raid
June 19

"Dead bodies were piled up near the Bank of Japan and Shizuoka Bank's Main Office. Americans dumped oil from planes and surrounded the city with fire bombs. An ocean of fire spread from the station all the way to the Gofuku shopping area. Two of my cousins were hit by a fire bomb and died on the spot. Fire bombs fell like heavy rain."

Fire at Shizuoka Station area on June 20

"My mother carried me on her back and ran around through the burning city without noticing that her kimono was on fire. If no one had noticed it and told my mother, I would have been burned alive."

Sasebo Air Raid   June 28

"On June 28, 1945, the air raid on Sasebo burned down the whole area from the station to Shimase Park. I saw many people whose bodies were swollen with severe burns."

"Americans surrounded the populated areas with bombs so that no one could escape, but they didn't drop bombs on useful buildings such as shipyards."

Many civilians were killed by U.S. bombings called "Tanabata(Star Festival Day) Air Raid" on July 7. Machine guns were fired outside of the city and fire bombs were dropped inside(Chiba City)

Kofu Air Raid   July 6

"On July 6, 1945, the sight of the area around Kofu Station Park was like a living hell. It started around 10 pm. Flare bombs fell upon the city with a cracking sound like mixing upmah-jong tiles. Then numerous fire bombs fell and surrounded the city which was caught in a sea of fire instantly. The moat around Maizuru Castle was filled with dead bodies. It truly was a living hell."

Chiba Air Raid   June 10, July 7

"We had evacuated from Tokyo to Chiba for safety, however, the Chiba air raid killed my mother and one sister and I was left with my two younger sisters and my brother."

Map of the area bombed by B-29s. It shows the large area around Chiba Station destroyed.

Seikan Ferryboats Targeted
July: Firing machine guns from fighter planes over the burnt city

"Just like atomic bombs, nearly 1000 people were massacred in Sendai." The city kept burning into the next morning. Volunteer guards in front.

Sendai Air Raid July 10

"Sendai was raided from the air on July 9, 1945. At the time I was in my 2nd year in high school. Americans dumped oil that night and dropped fire bombs, burning the entire city to the ground. The next morning I saw a lot of charred bodies lying all over."

"I was evacuated from Tokyo two years after the Great Air Raid. They moved us to Sendai, which was also later destroyed by fire. The inner circle of the city streetcar lines was all shuttered."

"I can still remember seeing the red sky over Sendai from the shelter, I was on my mother's back. I could see the prefectural and city buildings which were 2 km away from Sendai Station."

Utsunomiya Air Raid July 12

"Utsunomiya was also attacked badly. American fighters were firing machine guns during the day, they even fired at us, elementary school children. I rushed into a shelter. The fighter planes flew so low that I could clearly see the pilot with black sunglasses. My friend, on the way to a shelter, was hit right on the head by a fire bomb and burnt black. A baby in a stroller was shot and crippled. I was constantly trembling with fear. I have nightmares even now."

Hokkaido July 14-15

"In Hakodate ferryboats across Tsugaru Strait were attacked and sunk by U.S. fighters. One boat in flames rammed into the port deck and all the passengers and crew were killed. Not many people know about this, but it was awful."

"Hakodate was also attacked from the air and the area near the station was destroyed. I was staying with my brothers at a relative's house in Aomori, we had hardly enough food. After the war we tried to go back to Hakodate, Hokkaido, but were stuck at Aomori Port since all the ferries were destroyed."

Seikan ferryboats were attacked one by one. Almost all 13 boats were destroyed.

Aomori Air Raid July 28

Fire bombs were dropped in Aomori and destroyed the area around Aomori Station. They surrounded the city with bombs, gathered the citizens in the city center and massacred them.

Yonago Air Raid July 25

"I didn't want to volunteer to fight at the age of 19, so I chose to work at an air field. It was attacked. I was trembling and shuddering with fear inside the shelter when I saw a Grumman flying by us. One time 108 bombs were dropped. Mothers from the local women's groups were mobilized for a rescue mission. They gathered at the station to get on a train, which was later bombed and killed many women. Bodies were badly damaged and couldn't be easily identified, the husbands or other family members used clothing as a clue, collected the remains in bags, and cremated them on the river bank. "

August : Air Raids Continue till near the End of the War

Kumamoto Air Raid   July-August

"Kumamoto was attacked twice in July and August. The shopping district of Shimo-dori St. was the worst. Everything except for Kumamoto Castle was mostly destroyed. The city of Kumamoto was filled with bleeding people shot by machine guns."

Mito Air Raid   August 1

"80% of Mito city, from Mito station to Daiku City, was burned down. Only the Ibaragi Newspaper building and a department store survived. When I was in the 3rd grade, Hitachinaka city was engulfed in a heavy naval bombardment. I will never forget the fear I felt on that rainy night."

"Americans surrounded the city with fire-bombs so that no one could escape, then bombed the inside."

Maebashi Air Raid   August 5

"Because of the Nakashima Airfield and a plant manufacturing Zero fighters, the central part of Maebashi city was burned to the ground with fire bombs, leaving only a steel-framed department store. Shelters on the Hirose riverbank were attacked and the civilians inside were burnt to death. It was right before the end of the war."

Toyokawa Naval Factory   August 8

Female student volunteers at the navy factory.

"The naval factory in Toyokawa was attacked fiercely by 200 B-29's and 150 fighters. Inside the factory were mostly school-age girls and boys."

"2700 people were killed by this air-raid within 20 minutes."

Niigata Prefecture   August 10

"Niigata city did not experience terrible air-raids, but mines dropped in the nearby port like rain. Once, a ferryboat crossing Shinano River was bombed, killing all of the Niigata Commercial High School students on board."

Oita Prefecture   August 10

"It was burned and leveled to the ground. I could see the faraway ocean from the train station."

Miyazaki Prefecture   August 12

"In this area all but the city hall was burned down. Miyazaki city was bombed on August 12, just before the end of the war. The military headquarters located there was the target. American fighter planes flew so low that we could see the faces of the pilots."

Nagano Prefecture   August 13

"Nagano was a major target because of Matsushiro Daihonei (Imperial Headquarters) and an airfield. Gas tanks were bombed, and I saw a mother killed by a machine gun while she was hanging out diapers. B-29s flew over us the day before the end of the war. Through the end, Americans continued bombing hospitals."

Akita Prefecture
August 14

"The so-called 'last air-raid on Japan' destroyed the oil refinery in Tsuchizaki District."

Devastation of Kumamoto city. Kumamoto Castle and the surrounding woods are seen above.

The Mito Post Office Square was destroyed after the midnight air-raid on Aug. 1.

Toyokawa Naval Factory was completely burned down.

Citizen Witnesses of U.S. Air Raids on Shimonoseki City

Testimonies gathered in various places by the National Campaign Caravan for the Atomic Bomb Exhibition

Irie-cho and Maruyama-cho were completely burned down.

The Kanmon Straits, where you could see vessels damaged or sunk by the mines the U.S. dropped.

Survivors of atomic bombing and air raid talking about their experiences at the exhibition "Atomic bomb and Shimonoseki air raid" in November 2005.

Air-raid Alarms Day after Day

Mines-dropping began from the spring to the day of defeat in the 20th year of Showa

B29s dropped a tremendous number of mines.

In the 19th year of Showa (1944), a U.S. airplane was shot down, and a pilot bailed out in a parachute, landing somewhere near the fortress on the north side of Sako-machi. I went to see there along with the adults.

I saw an American soldier blindfolded with his hands bound behind him being hauled away in a truck.

(Owner, Fujinaga Clothing Store, Hikoshima)

Students are digging trenches.

From spring of the 20th year of Showa (1945), air-raid alarms were sounded everyday. B29s and other bombers dropped a tremendous number of mines in the Straits of Kanmon. All ships made of iron, even small coasters, were hit by those magnetic mines. Off the coasts along Nabe, Hosoe, Takezaki, and Hikoshima, the sea was jammed with sunken ships. Many sailors were killed. Some mines was dropped on the ground and the explosions killed and injured people around Uejo. Shimonoseki had been greatly damaged in the war before the fire-bombing.

(Okuno Mitsuo, Nabe-cho)

The Strait of Kanmon was the Key Target of "Operation Starvation"

Five thousand mines (one-half of all mines dropped in Japan) dropped in the Strait

The Strait of Kanmon. (U.S. forces photograph)

The Strait of Kanmon as seen from Moji.

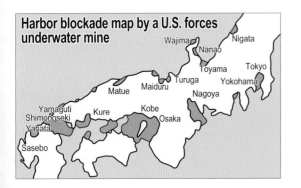

Harbor blockade map by a U.S. forces underwater mine

The mission was called "Operation Starvation." It was proposed by Admiral Nimitz to the U.S. Twenty-first Bomber Command to disrupt ①the import of materials and foods to Japan, ②Japanese logistics and troop movements, and ③Japanese shipping along the coasts.

The operation was combined with U.S. submarine efforts using torpedoes. The main target was set in and around the Kanmon Straits.

The straits were of high strategic importance because they were located at the intersection of several vital water routes, especially ones from the northern coasts of Kyushu and the Chinese Mainland.

"At the time we referred to it as Hosoe Bay, directly behind what was the Shimonoseki Police Station, the Hara Kohsan Building, which was San-yo Department Store at that time, and the Shimonoseki High Mart Building."

It was officially known as the "Hosoe Wharf." Ships went into the straits under the movable bridge along where the sidetracks of Japan Rail freight trains ran. To avoid the dangers of mines, coasters came there and were so jammed that we couldn't see water.

Later I learned that bombers dropped nearly 5,000 mines in the straits, half of all the mines U.S. dropped in the ports and bays of Japan. Everyday, ships touched mines and sank, with a bang, and big plumes of water.

I can only imagine that the damages Japan suffered of both ships and sailors were enormous. They continue to find mines in the straits when they dredge them, even now.   (Yasuda Kiyoshi , Hanano-cho)

Countless Dead Bodies Floated to the Coasts
Where Were They Buried?

The bodies of the sailors were left floating in the Strait of Kanmon.

U.S. bombers dropped mines into Kanmon Strait almost everyday. They flew lower than Mekari Hill, and dropped mines one after another.

The transport ships that had been anchored there overnight triggered the mines, exploded, and sank with a boom the next day when they tried to move. Afterward, the bodies of the sailors were left floating in the sea.

(Okano Mituo, Hosoe-cho)

A neglected grave : local people buried corpses of the crew of the ship which touched mine and sank.(Shimonoseki City Yoshimi)

Yasuda Kiyokazu & Co., which my father managed, dealt in fuel oil for ships. From around the spring of the 20th year of Showa (1945), when Japan would be defeated, U.S. bombers, B29s, dropped lots of mines in the Kanmon Strait. It was dreadful. It was already difficult that Japan transported foods and materials from the continent. Since the strait was a key point for Japanese coast guard, the U.S. moved to blockade the strait completely. Along the coasts of Shimonoseki and Moji, we saw masts of sunken ships reaching up out of the sea like trees.

(Yasuda Kiyoshi , Hanano-cho)

Though the Japanese Navy was Destroyed

Dropping the mines continued just before the defeat

Chikuma-maru sank in the Kanmon Straits.

"I think that there were many sinking brought by the explosion of the underwater mines, from the spring to the summer in 1945. Many ships under government service which were hit by the underwater mines, seem to have been cargo boats loaded with raw materials for the carrier and the factory of Kitakyushu in Japan. We salvaged sorghum, soy bean, and wheat, from the ship and ate them. They were in the sea, swelled up and were stinking, but we still had to eat them. In Moji district, I heard that many women waded into the sea up to their chest and took these cereals."

(Hikoshima Fujinaga clothing store)

Shiragi-maru. (Shimonoseki-Pusan ferry)

Toyo-maru. (merchant ship)

A motorized sailboat.

The second Karikawa-maru (884t) of Kawasaki Kisen hit a underwater mine at the Hikoshima Shiohama shore in Kanmon sea area on April 2 and sank. One hour after departing from Shimonoseki port, Kouan-maru (700t) a Kan-pu ferryboat fully loaded with 2,431 people, hit an underwater mine in the vicinity of Futaoijima and broke into pieces. After that, day after day, many ships were blown up and sank successively, and were often piled up. Ships hitting underwater mines totalled 500 cases. Besides navy ships, a motorized sailboat, a fishing boat, a merchant ship, a cargo boat to serve as the transportation as in Kan-pu ferryboat were being diverted to Saipan, at the time when main battleships were already lost. Approximately 350 ships have been recorded to be lost.

The number of victims, their birth, parentage, and burial are almost unknown.

The damage continued after the war, and the number of sinking by the underwater mines in the Kanmon barrier strait counted 12 ships by the end of 1945. Now, 2000 underwater mines were sunk into the bottom of the sea after "a declaration of safety" was announced, and the damage of dredging workboats continues to this day.

U.S. Forces Burned Down a City Area

More than 10,000 suffered but the death toll is unknown

On June 29 and July 2, it is an air raid twice in a city area
After precautionary warning cancellation, scattered oils and fats

A B29 U.S. military plane aimed twice at Shimonoseki in the daybreak of June 29 and July 2 1945. It dropped 420t (July 2, 360t) of incendiary bombs during the air raid on the city area. In addition, it burnt down the whole city residential area, 1,089,000 square meters equal to the center of Shimonoseki, 46,000 people were burnt out and more than 10,000 buildings burnt. But the known number of dead people is not clear.

B29 did "carpet bombing" by an incendiary from the warehouse area to the city area in Mojikou on June 29. It was called Shimonoseki air raid and was concentrated in the eastern areas of Shimonoseki when the ship that anchored in Mojikou began to burn. The incendiary device of the United States Armed Forces was called "Morozoff Bakery" because a hexagonal iron pipe was packed with incendiary cases in a basket. The basket opens in the air and as the incendiary cases are scattered and dropped. The incendiaries burnt in sequence not only at a target building but also in the crowded places of the central city area. This damage was the most terrible. In addition, many people took a direct hit of a incendiary case of the hexagon, and died. Many gravestones in the temple were destroyed, too. The people trained as bucket brigades for fire prevention during anti-air raid drills, but it did not make sense. It seemed to be fireworks, but it soon became an inferno. Fires burnt exhaustively around city areas of Amidaji-cho, Nakano-cho, Karato-cho, Akama-cho, Inari-machi, Nishino-hashi, Miyata-machi, Kihune-cho, Okushoji, Tanaka-machi, and the southeast district. "The second carpet bombing" with incendiary devices on July 2 aimed at the city central area of Shimonoseki and warehouses. I was able to look right across the city, across the flattened burnt stretches of land. Bad smoke still appeared around the city and it could be filled with the smell of burnt people in those days. Bloated dead bodies which swelled up stayed in the area. The external form of the iron concrete bank building would be left. The scene was much miserable. (Nabe-cho, Okuno Mituo)

A view of the Kanmon Straits from the fire-devastated area.

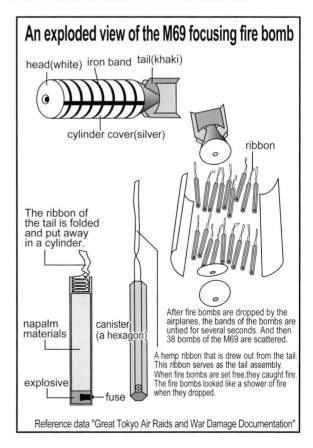

Moving Targets Were All Shot
Machine-gun fire from low-altitude planes

The U.S. carrier-based aircraft Grumman.

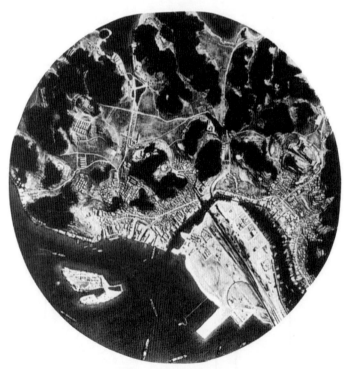

Kanmon District model which U.S. military made.

A carrier-based aircraft Grumman flew in and machine-gunned the area. I was in sixth grade in elementary school. When I was swimming at Maeda beach, I could see a Grumman pilot laughing as he shot at us.

(Masami Yamamoto, Maeda)

One day when Grumman fighters attacked the Moji district, I was surprised that I could see the individual faces of the pilots. I thought, "Damn these people. I will get my revenge!"

(Susumu Tokumura, Yamanokuchi)

I was sent to the Ohtake corps as part of the student mobilization. I worked for the maintenance of Imperial Navy fleet base in Iwakuni (now the U.S. Marine Corps base in Iwakuni). It was here that I was attacked by the U.S. carrier-based aircraft Grumman. The U.S. forces probably planned to take over the base. The Grumman plane machine-gunned people but did not drop bombs. Soldiers knew how to run from the machine-gun shootings but mobilized students fled everywhere. Many of my school friends were killed. Grumman attacks were kept continuing.

(Teruo Shibazaki, Hikoshima)

The Armed Forces and Mitsubishi Were Unharmed

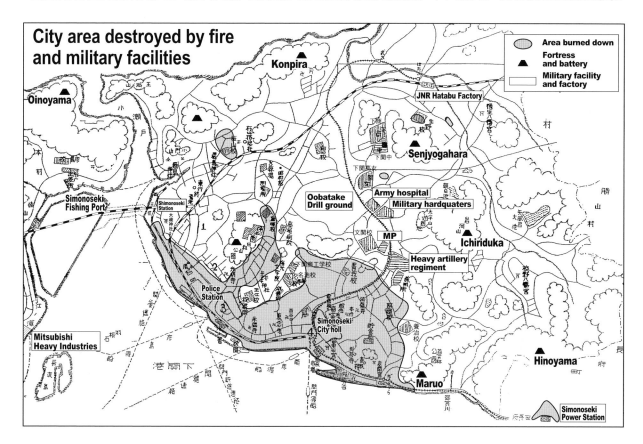

From a remark of Mitsubishi Zaibatsu supreme commander, Koyata Iwasaki

Mitsubishi has co-operated with many U.S. and British people in our business. Until today, they cooperated as our friends and held the same interest. Now the war happened, and we have become unhappy. However, the friendship we have long shared does not have to die. As long as Nation Law allows it, their personal lives and principles should be morally supported. If one day, peace comes again, we can become good friends again as it has been in the past. Thus, I hope for world peace and a time when humans help each other again.

(On December 10, 1941, inside meeting of the Zaibatsu)

The Japanese defeat was already decided. Why did they have to fire bomb the houses of civilians? I couldn't understand it. Neither the Shimonoseki heavy artillery regiment nor the military police headquarters, but now a library, were burnt down. We were forced to evacuate the Kihune region containing the Tanaka River, but it did not burn. It was strange that they said we were attacked because there was a fortress in Shimonoseki. There was a heavy artillery regiment, and there was a fortress too, but they were just there and were of no use to us. In order to make it easy to occupy Japan, the American Forces murdered many Japanese people. I understood this later, but Mitsui of Hikoshima and the Mitsubishi factory did not burn down either. The American forces did everything they were doing deliberately. (Shinmachi / Suwako Miyoshi)

Mitsubishi suffered no casualties in Hiroshima and Nagasaki.

When the U.S. armed forces dropped atomic bombs on Hiroshima and Nagasaki, they excluded particular targets of attack, including the Hiroshima shipyard of Mitsubishi Heavy Industries, the Hiroshima Machine Works, the Nagasaki shipyard of Mitsubishi Heavy Industries, and the Nagasaki Works of Mitsubishi Electric.

They Burned and Killed Civilians like Worms for Their Ambition to Rule Japan after the War

"Why is it wrong to attack civilians' homes?"

The death toll from the air raid on Tokyo	100,000 people
The death toll from the air raids on the whole country apart from Tokyo	80,000 people
Hiroshima	247,000 people
Nagasaki	150,000 people
Okinawa	187,000 people
Total	764,000 people
The death toll in China	710,000 people
The death toll in the south	1,317,100 people

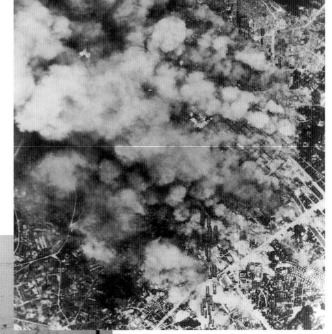

U.S. armed forces dropped fire bombs on the city going up in flames again.(Yokohama City)

A lot of corpses were left after an air raid. (Kobe City)

A selection of quotations from the reports and speeches of U.S. Maj. Gen. Curtis LeMay who directed the indiscriminate air raids on Japan as the Chief of the U.S. XXI

On Dec. 8, 1964, the Japanese Emperor conferred the First Order of Merit with the Grand Cordon of the Rising Sun upon Maj. Gen. Curtis LeMay

"I have to draw attention to the fact that our task was not supposed to indiscriminately bomb ordinary citizens. It was to destroy industrial and strategic targets."

"I didn't kill Japanese civilians. I destroyed Japanese munitions factories. All the civilians' houses in the Japanese cities were munitions factories. If one house was producing bolts, the next door house was making nuts. And the opposite house was making washers. Each civilian house made of wood and paper was a munitions factory producing weapons against us. Why is it wrong to attack them?"

"To shed the blood of people by using nuclear weapons is not more vicious than to split a human head by a rock."

"The deaths caused militarily does not add anything new to the notion of death. From the night of March 9 to the dawn of the next day, we burned to death more people in Tokyo than those who were vaporized in Hiroshima and Nagasaki."

There were no more miserable city than Hamamatsu. When our B29s dropped bombs because of being bombed by Japanese army and others, they were ordered to dispose of loaded bombs over Hamamatsu City.

The Truth about the Battle of Okinawa

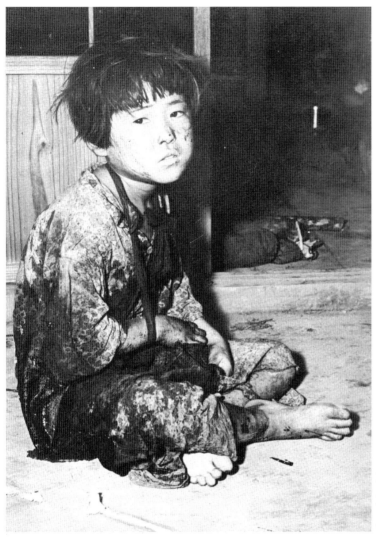

The real experiences of 1,000 Okinawans who suffered during the battle

The National Campaign Caravan for the Atomic Bomb Exhibition stated its itinerary in February 2004, and kept on holding outdoor exhibitions from Hokkaido in the north to Okinawa in the south. It went to Okinawa for the period September through November and met 1,000 Okinawans who told the truth about the Battle of Okinawa.

Separated from his family, this boy was left behind alone after a bombing run by U.S. warplanes. He disguised himself by wearing girl's clothes hoping to avoid possible disaster.

A woman talks about a wound that she received during the war. A shell splinter went through her right leg and left a deep scar.

When 1,500 Vessels and 550,000 U. S. Forces Attacked, the Naval Gun Attack was so Strong it Changed the Shape of the Land

Okinawa became a heap of debris from the bombardment by the warships of the U.S. Armed Forces.

More than 1,500 U.S. Armed Forces vessels which flocked in the Yomitan-son Hija River mouth continued bombardment form the warships for three months. The naval gun attack was so intense it changed the shape of the land.

Commander-in-Chief Halsey, who took command of the U.S. fleet during the battle in Okinawa, said "KILL JAPS, KILL JAPS, KILL MORE JAPS. You will help to kill the yellow bastards if you do your job well ."

Major General LeMay, who was the originator of carpet bombing that set fire to all the city, said "We will overthrow Japan and make it go back to a dark age."

The U.S. Army killed them. When we were walking on a footpath between the rice fields, we thought that a dead body was there when we saw a torn off foot. Even now, I am haunted by the moans of that dead person.

I was around 8 years old at the time. I ran away barefoot. When a bombardment of bombs came from a warship, they fell down like rain in pieces of sharp iron. I still have scars. I didn't like wearing shorts when I was in Elementary School. Even now, there are many people who received shoulder injuries from the warship bombardment who still feel the after-effects such as having difficulties breathing.

(A lady in her seventies)

War potential in the battle in Okinawa

U.S. armed forces
Aircraft carrier 16 boats   Battleship 8 boats   Number of soldiers
Cruiser 16 boats   Destroyer dozens of boats   A landing force, etc. 180,000 people
Troopship, etc.   Total 1500 boats   Total   550,000 people

Imperial Japanese Army
The army   86,400 people
The navy   about 10,000 people   } Total about 120,000 people
Defense forces and student
unit recruited in the field   about 20,000 people

The number of war deaths
Side of Japan Soldiers from the mainland   65,000 people
               Soldiers and civilian personnel from Okinawa   28,000 people } Total 187,000 people
               Public   94,000 people
U.S. armed forces   12,520 people

From Okinawa Relief Division.

The U.S. fleet which rained cannon-balls upon Okinawa Island.

U.S. Forces Slaughtered the Citizens of the Prefecture Indiscriminately

A family which escaped walking endlessly.

Inhabitants of the southern part of the Island annihilated by the bombardment of the U.S. Armed Forces.

"People from the south ran north and people from the north ran south in utter confusion. In the end, there was no safe place. Even in the trenches, bombs and flares could be fired so we didn't know where to run to."

American Grumman planes flew by at low altitudes. I ran away with a group of ten others, and they started to shoot at us, killing half of us. In the end, I hid in a cave which faced the sea. There was a person there who was suffering terribly and jumped headfirst into the sea to die. A soldier and a local person died as well. It was horrible. (Woman in her 70's)

In the Onaga district of Nishihara-cho, the number of the prewar households totaled 186, but the families of 71 houses were wiped out. Of a population of 886 people, 556 died. The reason so many families were annihilated is said to be that poison gas was used.

Warships bombed from the sea and machine-guns attacked from the sky.

They dropped gasoline-filled drums and then bombs.

The malaria and lice were the fault of the Americans.

A Spy plane sprinkled lice in Naha.

Flame throwers were fired, while grenades and poison gas were thrown into the trenches where the inhabitants hid.

A very young child who was killed by the indiscriminate carpet bombing of the U.S. Armed Forces and was left unattended.

The U.S. Armed Forces soldiers which marched while breaking down private houses.

In Deep Mourning for the Soldiers Abandoned in Okinawa

A Japanese soldier and a mobilized schoolgirl who escaped along the beach.

A Japanese soldier who forced a belly landing in the Yomitan-son airport occupied by the U.S. Armed Forces. He destroyed 7 U.S. military planes, damaged 20 planes and was shot dead.

Japanese soldiers undressed in a camp.

In the Deigo Tower, the ashes of about 500 members of charge corps are entombed. Community members and the bereaved continue a memorial service for 60 years.

"I'm sure Japanese militarism was wrong, but it doesn't mean the U.S. fought for the cause of justice or that the U.S. army behaved in a more responsible way than the Japanese. In fact, American soldiers were a lot crueler. I believe Americans killed a lot of unarmed citizens as well as soldiers, though some reformists say that Japanese were worse."

"My brother signed up for the army of his own will, only to die in service. Actually so many soldiers like him were killed in that war. I'm very sorry this fact is neglected."

"Some of the soldiers from the mainland stayed with us, crammed into my house. They had little food for themselves. My mother gave potatoes to one soldier after another. She also made rice porridge for the soldiers suffering from diarrhea. They appreciated her kindness very much. Later I saw them beaten by a senior officer."

"Combat planes of a suicide corps flew over our village and crashed into the U.S. army. I felt deep sorrow for the poor pilots, wondering what they had been like. They sacrificed their lives to save us."

"Knowing the troops in Okinawa chose to die an honorable death, the commanding officer, Yusuke Koike, who was also a medical officer, gave a speech. He said we would never have a terrible war like this again. He hoped we would survive and pass the tragic story of the war on to the younger generation. He gave each of us a sack of hard and dry biscuits, a small piece of dried bonito, and a can of beef. Then he shook hands with us, saying goodbye. After that I heard he killed himself with dignity."

"I too Survived Naval Guns"
Wishes of the Survivors

Mobilized students providing first aid to each other under the surveillance of U.S. soldiers.

We met with so many people who cried as they told us.

"Four people out of six in my family were killed at the same time."

"My father was shot to death by an American soldier in front of me when we were escaping from the attack."

"My sister's friend was raped and killed by American soldiers."

Yaka Camp U.S. forces fiercely attacked the residents with naval guns, continuing their attack onto land and driving people into camps. They confiscated the land and built bases.

"As it was said after the War that if Japanese militarism had won the war, the situation would have been more terrible, it was difficult to talk about the was crimes of the U.S. Though the true enemy was the U.S., people of mainland Japan have been considered as ors enemy. In the same way as fellow at time of the Korean War, this is the American way to make Japanese fight each other."

I don't want any stuff-based happiness from the U.S. military. I want the happiness of a true heart. I want to live a self-sufficient life by agriculture and fishery, and get rich of the U.S. bases. And I want to tell the truth of the Battle of Okinawa to a new young generation."

People held at gunpoint by U.S. soldiers after being found hiding in a cave.

"Koza Riot" (1970) Recounted Proudly

Bar hostesses played an active role

Koza Riot" (present day Okinawa City) December 20, 1970.

Looking back at the "Koza Riot," which occurred in Koza City (present Okinawa City) in 1970, many people express surprisingly their anger toward the extremely high-handed American colonial rule throughout the post-war period. Voices full of pride reflect the then ever-growing movement to restore Okinawa to Japan's control.

Vehicles of U.S. soldiers torched during the Koza Riot which incited the long-standing anger of the people towards the U.S. Army.

"A car accident involving members of the U.S. military and a local man in Koza triggered the riot. During the disturbance, people set fire to cars with 'Y' license plates (plates for American military personnel) one after another. Local youths were at the front of the street fight, and barmaids at the back. The hostesses who had suffered profound humiliation at bars exclusive to white American servicemen supplied empty beer bottles. They blew off steam by cheering on the youngsters, shouting 'Hurl these bottles at them!'"

The American army could not fire at local civilians. Several protesters were arrested, charged with causing disturbance in a public place, but were found innocent afterward. People in Koza might have been dependent economically on the American military bases, but they were brave enough to challenge the soldiers when it came to the crunch. They kept their pride intact even while suffering humiliation.

(From a man in his 60s)

20,000 base workers entered into a strike of 24 hours. They bravely confronted U.S. soldiers who wielded bayonets. June 5, 1969.

"American soldiers leveled guns at us when President Eisenhower visited Okinawa in 1960. But we never flinched at that. I was so moved by the dignified manner of the Zen - Gun - Ro (All Okinawa Garrison Forces Labor Union) workers confronted by the soldiers with bayonets. Workers took a stand against the continuing presence of U.S. military bases in Okinawa."

(Man, 75 years old)

Massacre to Obtain Military Bases

‒ Occupation of Okinawa and Japan planned as early as after the Russo ‒ Japanese war

Battle of Okinawa

The code name for the battle of Okinawa was "Operation Iceberg." The United States intended that battle to release Okinawa from Japanese control and set up military bases to secure air and sea control of the region. Okinawa would serve as a springboard for the planned invasion of China as well as the Japanese mainland.

In April, when the attack on Okinawa began, commander Buckner said "We should control this island as a 'protectorate,' 'mandate,' or some other name, providing us with Okinawa as a means of access to the China sea and as an outpost to prevent Russia from expanding into the Pacific from Chinese ports. In July, army general George C. Marshall said "the Yellow Sea and its surrounding regions will be among the disputed areas after the war. For this reason it is desirable to deploy American forces at Ryukyu islands and leave other demilitarized areas to friendly countries."

Forty thousand copies of an extra edition of Chosyu Shinbun, that was distributed in Okinawa, aroused shock and sympathy from a lot of people.

Plan Orange ‒ The invasion of Japan

As early as 1906, immediately following the Russo-Japanese war, the United States had developed a war strategy with Japan, which they code-named "Plan Orange." One of the drafters of the policy, Dewey, wrote: "Though the United States carries the banner of pacifism, if attacked especially on Hawaii by Japan, people would stand up with anger, endure war, and launch a counter-attack making the best use of industrial power to bring Japanese military and economic power to an end with unconditional surrender."

Don't attack the Imperial Palace. We can make use of the emperor.

The "Japan Plan" decided by the Division of Psychological Operations of the Department of Military Intelligence of U.S. Army was discovered at National Archives and Records Administration recently. The "Japan Plan" was launched to frame immediately after the Japanese assault on Pearl Harbor in December 1941. This plan specified the strategy to utilize the emperor as a symbol of peace. And it schemed to push all war responsibility off onto the "military," to decriminalize the emperor, and to occupy and control Japan under a system that recognized the emperor as a symbol of the state.

The U.S. government came out with the joint plan of a guiding principle between the U.S. and the United Kingdom in May 1942. The plan wrote clearly that all attacks of the Imperial Household had to be avoided. And the U.S. government carried out the order to prohibit the bombing to the Imperial Palace on the occasion of the savage air raid on Tokyo.

At the time, Mr. Reischauer, who became U.S. ambassador to Japan after the war, suggested establishing "a puppet government centering on Hirohito" after the victory of the war between the U.S. and Japan. He asserted that the emperor was equal to one million American forces stationed in Japan.

Atomic bombs and poems of Sankichi Toge

An Appeal of All Voices from Under the Atomic Cloud

An Appeal of All Voices
(Excerpts)

Sankichi Toge

Portrait of Sankichi Toge (1917~1953)

When you see the clouds burning in a blue sky,
When you find the asphalt roads softened by the heat,
When you smell weeds and dust in the wind,
I want you to know through this collection of poems*
That seven years after the war,
Tired by the life without any signs of bright prospects,
People of Hiroshima
Recall suddenly their feelings of those days
Hear those cries coming from within the flames and under the rubble
And repress their anger by quivering their clenched fists stealthily as they don't know what to do with it.

People of Hiroshima, and of Nagasaki
Trying to get out of the atomic flames and recover themselves
Still struggle desperately
Under the deceptive strength of the atomic bombs.
Even by struggling
We,
With the sense of our skins which have soaked up those flames and bloody pus,
And with our bodies covered with tears we have shed for our beloved wives, children and parents lost under the mushroom cloud,
Now come to know.

Ah, then we can know.
By the yellow skin of the Japanese on whom the atomic bombs were dropped for the first time in the world,
And by the jet-black pupils and streaming black hairs,
We can know
That we should carry out the fight for peace
Arm in arm
With all peoples in the world who love the truth and labor
Except a mere handful of men who want wars for satisfying their worldly desires and maintaining their power
And don't deserve to be called human being.
This is now already the only way of realizing
Our desire as human being to make an honest and happy life.
As Japanese
And as Asians
We can know that.
For that,
Yes, in order to believe that,
By overcoming much unspeakable pain
And by taking much risk in speaking,
All people
Including aged men, housewives, widows, youths
And children guided by brave teachers
Raise their cries covered with blood and tears
Through this collection of poems.

I wish
This trust and love
To achieve great results
In the innumerable voices hating wars and cursing atomic bombs.
May the cries from the underground
Which are hidden under those voices and will never cease but exist for ever
Be healed by the strength of living ourselves!
May those who design to use atomic bombs
Be extinguished as early as possible
By the strength of the working people all over the world
Before dropping again atomic bombs on the ground!

From *"Poems about the Atomic Bomb Found in a Wicker Trunk"*
*"*From under the Atomic Cloud,"* a book with poems of children, edited by Sankichi Toge and his friends and published in 1952.

Who Could Forget That Flash!

Hiroshima (August 6, 1945)
2 or 3 minutes after the explosion, a column of cloud with strange color rose high in the sky. (7km east-northeast of the hypocenter. Photograph by Seizo Yamada)

Nagasaki (August 9, 1945)
10minutes after the explosion, a mushroom cloud was seen from the Kawanami Shipyard in the Koyagi Island, about 10 km southwest of the hypocenter. The first photograph taken on the ground. (Photograph by Hiromichi Matsuda)

Hiroshima (August 6, 1945)
A photograph taken from one of the three B-29s which participated in the bombing attack, about 80 km from the hypocenter, at an altitude of 12,000 m.

At 8:15 a.m. on August 6th, 1945
The first bomb of Uranium 235 in the world
Was dropped on Hiroshima.
At 11 a.m. on the 9th of this month
The bomb of Plutonium was dropped on Nagasaki.
In Hiroshima, out of its population of 400,000, 247,000 lives were claimed.
It is said that the atomic bomb only is never so militarily powerful as to decide the war.
But why did it bring about such a tragic reality?
It was dropped on unarmed citizens of Hiroshima
And on a religious area near the downtown of Nagasaki
At a time when the most of the citizens were rounded up in the central parts of the cities just as the cattle in a slaughterhouse.
Everything had been planned very well.

Excerpts from *"An Appeal of All Voices"* Sankichi Toge

What Were under the Atomic Cloud ?

Hiroshima City before the atomic bombing. The dome of the Hiroshima Prefectural Industrial Promotion Hall (now called A-bomb Dome) is seen on the left. (Photograph by Noboru Watanabe)

Hondori Shopping Arcade in Hiroshima before World War II. (Courtesy Hiroshima Municipal Archives)

A corner of the Hama-machi Streetcar Street in Nagasaki before the War.

What were under that mushroom cloud?
There were
Schools, hospitals, government offices, banks, churches and stores.
All of them were destroyed.
But many of the munitions plants
Outside the sea of flames
Were almost undamaged
Except for some windows, doors and ceilings.
In deed, the National Railways recovered its function in three days.
Those who died in that sea of flames were
Young and old citizens including employees, students and children.
There were also soldiers, but weak ones remaining in the exhausted military.

The center of this Hiroshima City was frail like a baby bird.
At that chosen time
Hiroshima had a naive look.
In the Hiroshima Central Post Office at the hypocenter
It was the time of changing from the night shift to the day shift.
The whole work force was inside the office and that old-fashioned brick building was filled with 600 workers.
Only an old janitor
Went outside to throw away garbage in a can beside the front door.
In the Western Military Drill Ground, 700 or 800 meters northeast of the hypocenter
It was just the time when a group of uniformed soldiers who were drafted into the army that morning lined up
While their families with small national flags in hands were seeing them wistfully.

In the Prefectural Office, 1,000 meters from the hypocenter
Workers came to work to relieve 200 persons on night watch, who went back home.
Then a group of mobilized female students were walking in a corridor
With cleaning buckets in hands.

In the Zakoba district behind the City Hall, about 1,500 meters from the hypocenter
Hundreds of first- and second-year students of the Prefectural Girls' High School, First Prefectural Middle School, Second Municipal Middle School and other schools started their work
According to their teachers' instructions
To clean the sites of demolished houses.
In the same district or in the Dobashi district at the same distance from the hypocenter
Elderly people and housewives with babies on their back,
Who were mobilized to do the same work through neighborhood associations and volunteers' units from various districts around the city,
Wiping sweat,
Gathered to start the work.

A narrow shopping mall of the Yokogawa district, 2,000 meters from the hypocenter
Was filled with large crowds of people commuting from the suburbs to the city.
In a number of houses, 3,000 meters from the hypocenter
Aged people and little children were about to clear the table or wash the dishes after they ate breakfast and sent other family members to the working sites or workshops.

Excerpts from *"An Appeal of All Voices"* Sankichi Toge

One Instat Swept Thirty Thousand Off the Street

Hiroshima (A little after 11 a.m., August 6, 1945) : The first photograph taken on the ground, at the west end of the Miyuki Bridge, about 2.3 km from the hypocenter. The two sidewalks on the bridge were filled with dead or wounded people. (Photograph by Yoshito Matsushige)

In the spring and summer of 1945
Many cities all over Japan were burned out every night.

It was said that bills were dropped from the sky in the evening of August 5th
To inform that Hiroshima would be burned away at last.
Because of the rumors which had been spread a couple of days before
Many of the citizens fled to nearby hills or fields
And passed an anxious night
Under the galaxy in the pitch dark sky.
In the middle of the night, 200 B29s flied over the Bungo Channel and intruded on the airspace of the Hiroshima Bay. They circled round in the sky for tens of minutes,
Pretending to make a raid on Hiroshima.
But suddenly they took a southwesterly course
And flied away toward Hikari City.
The air-raid alarm was canceled at dawn.
The radio informed that four enemy planes were in the airspace of Hiroshima Prefecture, but soon they flied away.
Even the preliminary warning was canceled at 7:50 a.m.
At that time, many citizens heard the roar of B29s.
But who could know
That American crew members with dark glasses
On board three warplanes carrying the shame of the human being
Were penetrating at a high altitude?
The citizens felt quite relieved as nothing happened last night.
They went back home to have a quick breakfast.
After that, the employees left for their workshops, the students went to school and then to their working sites,
And the mobilized members of the neighborhood associations in the suburbs moved from their towns and villages to the center of Hiroshima.
It was the time when the biggest number of the citizens were out of doors
As if things were precisely calculated on the basis of the statistics.

Excerpts from *"An Appeal of All Voices"* Sankichi Toge

Hiroshima (About 5 p.m., August 6, 1945) At the corner of a streetcar stop in Minami-machi, 2.4 km south-southeast of the hypocenter. A policeman writing out disaster certificates for citizens. (Photograph by Yoshito Matsushige)

They Killed Children, Women and Working people

Hiroshima (About 11 a.m., August 6, 1945): A soldier gave a first aid treatment applying ointment to the burnt people who had fled to the Miyuki Bridge, escaping from the flames. Among them were many students of the Girls' Commercial School and First Prefectural Middle School who were exposed to the atomic bomb during their building demolition work. *(Photograph by Yoshito Matsushige)

Ah, in fear and trembling under the war regime
The docile Japanese people
Gave away their fathers, husbands and sons,
Abandoned all their valuables even diamond and gold
Always in obedience to the order of the men of power with the Emperor at the head,
Wrapped themselves in rags, crunched on soybeans and ate wild grass.
When they were exposing their foolishly naive expression
To the blue sky of August,
Such a tremendous energy
Stronger than the destructive power of 20,000 tons of TNT
And made of the solar energy now
Was radiated at a height of 500 meters.
The beam of light was so strong
That most of the children whose poems are collected in this book write about their impressions of the flash.
The color of the light varies from witness to witness.
They mention different colors ranging from red, violet, white, dark blue to orange.
Nonetheless the strong light took the eyesight from those who looked at it straight.
Tragedy of Hiroshima began at that moment.

Excerpts from "*An Appeal of All Voices*" Sankichi Toge

*The national government adopted the Urban Demolition Plan which targeted more than one hundred of locations in Hiroshima for destruction of homes and other buildings in order to create fire lanes

Hiroshima City in Flames

Hiroshima
(1 hour after the explosion, August 6, 1945)
The greater part of the city was in flames.
(From Ujina, 4.5 km from the hypocenter. Photograph by Gonichi Kimura)

Hiroshima (About 8:15 a.m., August 6, 1945)
Burning city and fleeing people near Kyobashi, about 1.4 km from the hypocenter.
(Drawn by Kazuhiro Ishizu, aged 37 in 1945. From *"Pictures about the Atomic Bomb Drawn by Citizens"*)

The Hiroshima Central Post Office,
Due to an unprecedented shock wave right down on it,
Collapsed in an instant, leaving all the workers dead.
Only the old janitor could survive, but he died a couple of days later.
In the Western Military Drill Ground, a whole group of soldiers were found dead with their bodies scattered.
Some were raw with no skin and some others were charred.
Those who escaped from being crushed to death in the Prefectural Office
Crawled on their hands and knees toward the riverbank
As they were eager for water.
At the west end of the Yorozuyo Bridge, there remained a pile of dead bodies undisposed for two days after the bomb.
That heap of bodies piled on the bottom of the river was higher than the riverbank.

Excerpts from *"An Appeal of All Voices"* Sankichi Toge

I'm Very Hot! Help Me!

Hiroshima (Soon after the explosion, August 6, 1945)
A mother was trying to make a hole to rescue her daughter from the burning house in Nishihakushima-cho, about 1.4 km from the hypocenter.
 (Drawn by Chiyoe Kagawa, aged 39 in 1945.
  From *"Pictures about the Atomic Bomb Drawn by Citizens"*)

Hiroshima (August 6, 1945)
Helping a girl seriously injured on the chest and covered with blood, I dashed through the fires desperately in Kojin-machi or Akebono-cho.
 (Drawn by Yoshiko Michitsuji, aged 19 in 1945.
  From *"Pictures about the Atomic Bomb Drawn by Citizens"*)

The same tragedy happened to the people staying at home.
Through openings in the instantly crushed houses
Arms were stretched out and continued to dig holes for escape
Until the last moment when the trapped people were caught by the flames.
"I'm very hot! Help me!" – The cry for help which had been continuing in a feeble voice stopped at last
Without getting the helping hand.
The whole city of Hiroshima was burned up in the fire and reduced to ashes.
There was no people to come back even for gathering the ashes.
Then, a heavy black rain began to fall in the northwestern part of the city
On the flames raising a gust of wind and bringing about whirlwinds.
A rainbow appeared and hung for a while on the hills of Koi.
Its color remains vividly in the memory of survivors.
  Excerpts from *"An Appeal of All Voices"* Sankichi Toge

Hordes of Wailing Naked

Hiroshima (August 6, 1945) : A teacher was taking a group of high-school girls, all naked, to the Koi Elementary School in the black rain.
(Drawn by Kishiro Nagara, aged 40 in 1945. From *"Pictures about the Atomic Bomb Drawn by Citizens"*)

How can we describe the end of those people?
Lower-grade students of middle schools and girls' high schools
Who were doing the clearance work after the demolition of homes
And teachers who were leading them.
Dressed in clothes they liked,
Some in new straw hats,
Singing songs and joking with each other,
The students arrived at the locations.
All were 13- or 14-year-old boys and girls.
All of a sudden, they were struck by a flash and blown down.
Those who barely stood up after the smoke cleared away
No longer had their beautiful image like flower.
Clothes were burned and torn up.
Skin was peeled off.
Flesh was exposed.
Faces were swollen.
Wounds were gaped as dropping stones and timbers hit them.
Calling for mother or teacher,
Even crawling on their hands and knees,
Students fled toward Mt. Hiji.
Many of the members of neighborhood associations from Dobashi district sustained burns.

Hiroshima (August 9, 1945)
With no one to help her, a girl died sitting on the bank of the Enko River.
(Drawn by Masato Yamashita, aged 21 in 1945. From *"Pictures about the Atomic Bomb Drawn by Citizens"*)

It was said that they slid down the bank of the Tenma River to cool their burnt bodies and escape from the fires
And were carried away by the stream.
But there was no full information about them.

Excerpts from *"An Appeal of All Voices"* Sankichi Toge

No Longer Their Beautiful Image Like Flower

Hiroshima (About 9:30 a.m., August 6, 1945)
Seriously wounded, middle-school students were in agony after having fled to Mt. Hiji, about 2.3 km from the hypocenter.
(Drawn by Toshifumi Goto, aged 20 in 1945. From *"Pictures about the Atomic Bomb Drawn by Citizens"*)

The flames over the city were brightly illuminating the sky even after night had fallen.
In the meantime, in the towns and villages neighboring the city of Hiroshima
Survivors thronged hospitals, schools, temples and private houses
Where they fell one upon another.
Vomiting blood from mouth and nose
They died one after another.
Those who died immediately turned into skeletons.
Those who were seriously burned died one after another within one or two weeks,
Covered with pus and maggots.
Innumerable flies bred some time in September.
The symptoms of the atomic bomb disease started to appear around August 20.
Unwounded survivors began to lose their hair and suffer from diarrhea, vomiting and fever.
They continued to vomit blood and died after spots appeared all over their bodies.
This irremediable disease
Seized on the survivors.
The medicines had run out already.
They needed nutritious food and fresh fruits.
But whoever could get such things at that time?
Even under this situation,
In some hospitals
Those who had money could undergo medical treatment as much as possible
While those who had no money nor relatives
Were left after simple treatment.

Excerpts from *"An Appeal of All Voices"* Sankichi Toge

Give Me Water! Water!

Hiroshima (About 9 a.m., August 7, 1945)
Schoolboys crowded into a water tank and died near the Aioi Bridge, about 300 m from the hypocenter.
 (Drawn by Kikue Komatsu, aged 37 in 1945.
 From *"Pictures about the Atomic Bomb Drawn by Citizens"*)

Hiroshima (August 6, 1945)
Dead bodies piled up on the bank and floating on the river near the Kouhei Bridge, about 2.3 km from the hypocenter.
(Drawn by Shinko Ishibashi and Harumi Nakagiri, respectively aged 7 and 31 in 1945. From *"Pictures about the Atomic Bomb Drawn by Citizens"*)

Little Brother

Hideo Kurusu, 5th grade
Funairi Elementary School, Hiroshima City

Between boards
My little brother is caught.
Groaning.
He said to me
Give me water, water.
I said
I don't like to go inside the fallen house.
He said nothing
And died in silence.
I should have brought him water.

From *"From under the Atomic Cloud"*

August 6th **Sankichi Toge**

Who could forget that flash!
One instant swept
Thirty thousand off the street,
Crushing darkness stifled
Fifty thousand screams,

Then yellow smoke whirling upwards
Reveals rent buildings and smashed bridges,
Crowded trams standing gutted
And interminable rubble and cinders.
This was Hiroshima.
Then there came, hands on breasts,
Shredded skin hanging,
Treading in spilt brains,
Singed tatters of cloth about their hips,
Hordes of wailing naked.

Bodies scattered like stone images over the parade ground;
A tangled mass crawled to moored timber rafts
And died in heaps under the parching sun.
Flames, soaring against the evening sky,
Burned alive
Mothers and brothers pinned under ruins.
In the faeces on the arsenal floor
Escaped schoolgirls
Sprawled, swollen-bellied,
Eyes shattered, skinless and hairless.
The morning sun shone on the unrecognizable herd.
Nothing moved,
In the hanging stench
But a cloud of flies round the metal basins.

Who could forget that total silence
That reigned over the city of three hundred thousand.
How could we forget the wishes
That our lost wives and children
Forced deep into our hearts
Through their bleached orbits of eyes
In that silence!

Stunned Silence Filling the Air

Nagasaki (August 10, 1945)
Near (only 110 m from) the hypocenter.
Charred bodies were seen here and there.
 (Photograph by Yosuke Yamahata)

Hiroshima (August 7, 1945)
Hondori business quarters,
500 m east of the hypocenter.
The ground was still hot.
 (Photograph by Mitsugu Kishida)

Hiroshima (August 12, 1945)
This streetcar was exposed to the A-bomb at the
Kamiya-cho junction, 250 m from the hypocenter.
Most of the passengers packing in it were charred.
 (Photograph by Yotsugi Kawahara)

Out of
Earth dimmed and
Canopied
By an unfurling shroud
Of dense hanging cloud;
Sweeping smoke
Growling, gnashing,
Rearing up
Into the cloud,
Flame – lurid
Violet dark
Over the city
Showering sparks
Towering up.

Like a mirage of weaving weed under cool water
An army of flames strode through the city.
Wings crumpled, a gray pigeon dropped
In the middle of the bridge.
A herd of cattle for the abattoir
Rolled like an avalanche
Down the bank of the river.
Beneath pouring fumes
Men on all-fours
Groped and crawled out
Only to be devoured by the fire.
Amid cinders in heaps
A curse smoulders,
Stands stiff,
Tearing its hair.

After that
Moment condensed
And exploded
Incandescent hatred
Filling the huge sky. Then
Stunned silence
Filling the air.

Excerpts from *"Flare"* Sankichi Toge

Why Have You Had to Suffer This?

Nagasaki (August 10, 1945)
The charred body of a boy in Iwakawa-machi, 700 m from the hypocenter.
(Photograph by Yosuke Yamahata)

No person to raise and embrace
Your murdered body.
No person to cover the shame of your burnt-away slacks.
No one to wipe away the mark of agony stuck there either.
You did your painful best
To struggle in your humble life
Always living with a shy quiet smile.
And you reached the most bashful age,
Suppressing the maiden dreams welling in your breast.

Then your soft buttocks were exposed to the sun;
Occasional passers-by searching among the bodies
Glanced absent-mindedly
At the dried stool.

Cruelty! Anguish! Tragedy!
NO!
More than this,
What shall we do about the shame?
You can no longer feel the shame,
Yet the shame burns into those who see it,
Stabs into the heart the more sharply
With the passing of time.
The shame has already left you, and is now
Graven into the whole Japanese people!

Excerpts from *"When Will the Day Come?"*
Sankichi Toge

Nagasaki (August 10, 1945)
The dead bodies of mother and child on the platform at the Urakami Railway Station, about 1 km from the hypocenter.
(Photograph by Yosuke Yamahata)

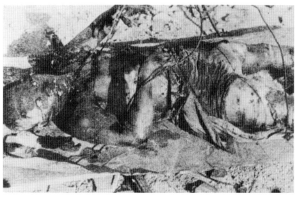

Hiroshima (August 12, 1945)
A soldier burned black in a drill ground.
(Photograph by Satsuo Nakata)

What Shall We Do about This Shame?

Nagasaki (August 10, 1945)
The A-bomb blast blew away a running streetcar and threw about passengers at 230 m from the hypocenter. The parts that look black in the dead bodies are actually deep red, the effect of burns from radiation.
(Photograph by Yosuke Yamahata)

Untitled
Mareomi Okano, 5th grade
Minamikannon Elementary School, Hiroshima City

My Mummy and I,
Thinking of coming back
To Hiroshima
From Nagasaki
Where we met relatives,
Got on a train.
We were in the train
When we saw the atomic bomb flash.
Aunty sitting next to me
Prayed, "Nam myou houren gekyou."
  (Note: This is a Buddhist pray meaning literally
   "Glory to the Sutra of the Lotus of the Supreme Law".)
When we arrived in Hiroshima
We saw dead bodies
Piled up
Near the station.
When we got to our house
We found the roof tiles
Blown off.
My Grandma who had been in quite good health
And lived with us
Was defeated this time
By Pikadon (atomic bomb)
My Grandma
Was killed
By Pikadon
An uncle of mine
In Nagasaki
Was killed too.

From *"From under the Atomic Cloud"*

Nagasaki
Only a soldier and a woman left dead in the streetcar which was full of passengers. The others were thrown out.
(Photograph by Yosuke Yamahata)

Nagasaki
(August 10, 1945)
A carriage and a horse in and around Iwakawa-machi, about 700 m south-southeast of the hypocenter.
(Photograph by Yosuke Yamahata)

Searching for Relatives, People Were Exposed to Radiation

Nagasaki (August 10, 1945) People entered the city to search for their relatives and acquaintances. (Near Sumiyoshi. Photograph by Yosuke Yamahata)

Nagasaki (August 10, 1945) They walked up and down in the city. (Near the Inasa Bridge. Photograph by Yosuke Yamahata)

Untitled
Masao Kagawa, 5th grade
Minamikannon Elementary School, Hiroshima City

After my big brother Yoshio was killed by the atomic bomb
My Mummy looked for him everyday and everyday.
But she couldn't find his clothes,
Nor his bag,
Nor his lunch box,
Nor his bones.
My Mummy said
Yoshio, why did you die?
She cried and cried.
I hate
Atomic bomb.

From *"From under the Atomic Cloud"*

Hiroshima (August 9, 1945) Rescue teams came also from the other prefectures of the Chugoku Region, even from the Kansai Region, and entered the city. (Near Kamiya-cho. Photograph by Mitsugu Kishida)

School Grounds Were Turned into Crematories

Hiroshima (August 8, 1945)
Bodies were gathered and cremated in the ground of the Honkawa Elementary School near the hypocenter, separated only by a river. (Photograph Toshio Kawamoto)

Hiroshima (August 10, 1945)
Rescuers bring bodies to a cremation site. (Photograph by Hajime Miyatake)

An Atomic Bomb

Hatsumi Sakamoto, 3rd grade
Hijiyama Elementary School,
Hiroshima City

When an atomic bomb falls
Day becomes night
And people become ghosts.

From *"From under the Atomic Cloud"*

Hiroshima (July 1952)
Seven years after the bombing, skeletons of victims were found in and around the city, for instance, near the former temporary relief center of the military in Saka Town, Aki County. Survivors had arrived there at last, but died one after another. 60 bodies had been left out in the open, covered with weeds and exposed to the weather, while 156 bodies had been buried. Skulls of young people with no decayed tooth moved the people to tears.

The Wounded Died One after Another

Warehouse Record
(Excerpts)

Sankichi Toge

That Day:

Most are junior schoolgirls lying crammed together like sardines. They had been clearing up the debris of evacuated houses. However, burns, mercurochrome, blood clots, ointment and wads of bandages have transformed them into a gang of beggarly old crones, fetid apparitions.

Besides walls and behind the thick pillars are pails or buckets full of vomit, urine, and faeces, some of it spilt over the floor. In the putrid pungent smell, their pleading voices are shrill, feeble, endless.

"Help, Daddy, help me!"
"Water, water! Ah, lovely water!"
"Fifty cents! Here is fifty cents!"
"Get this dead body away from my feet, please!"

Some are already wildly deranged, others motionless in death; but there is nobody to shift them. Distraught, questing parents wander in from time to time to scrutinize faces or patterns on girls' working slacks. They look ashen and very severe in their anti-air-raid clothing. Whenever the girls notice anybody coming in, their wailings rise to a hysteric unison of "Water! Water!"

(Continued on page 70)

Nagasaki (August 10, 1945)
Victims lie down on the road and wait for relief.
(Near Takara-machi. Photograph by Yosuke Yamahata)

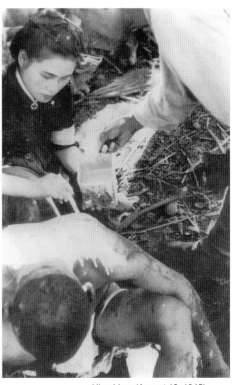

Hiroshima (August 12, 1945)
Victims laid on the truck.
(Photograph by Hajime Miyatake)

Nagasaki (About 3 p.m., August 10, 1945)
A nurse applies tincture of oil to a sufferer at a hurriedly built relief headquarters.
(Near the Michinoo Railway Station. Photograph by Yosuke Yamahata)

Their Condition Was Beyond Help

Hiroshima (August 7, 1945)
No medicine. Apply tincture of oil to the burnt face and put a piece of gauze on it. That was their best they could do. At a relief center in a tent of the Hiroshima Second Army Hospital, about 1.2 km from the hypocenter.
 (Photograph by Yotsugi Kawahara)

Nagasaki (August 10, 1945)
Michinoo, about 4 km north of the hypocenter, was the nearest railway station to the atom-bombed area. Trains could bring relief supplies and rescue teams to that station. Wounded people were lying on the straw mats spread in front of the station. These little children were so exhausted that they could not even cry. A relief team, with the help of some survivors, applied tincture of oil to them by a writing brush.
 (Photograph by Yosuke Yamahata)

(Continued from page 69)

The Second Day:
 A quiet morning, incredibly silent. Half the group on the floor have gone; there is none of yesterday's screaming. The survivors' bodies are green and bloated: their arms cannot be distinguished from their thighs, their thighs from their abdomens. Singed maiden hair, along with the charred remains of cranial hair and that in the armpits, deepens with shadow the hollows of mangled, distorted bodies. Only the slit, leaden eyes are distinguishable in this abyss of shadows.

The Third Day:
 Mrs K's condition: respiration 30, pulse 100. Burns cover one side of the face, the whole of the back and a little of the hips and the heels. High fever. No appetite. Eyes which were still and steady this morning staring at the others as they screamed, now gleam wildly. Hands shake as she squats over the excreta bucket gripping the rim. "Give me water! Give me a cup of tea! I want to have salted melon...." Towards evening delirium sets in.

The Fourth Day:
 Diarrhea severe and watery. Eyebrows scorched, eyelids distorted. No shadow of a smile. Burns all suppurating. The only medication available: ointment for burns, some herbs for diarrhea. Watery excrement now flecked with blood. Purple and crimson blotches beginning to show on the remaining skin.

(Continued on page 70)

Hiroshima (August 10, 1945)
A relief center of the Army Marine Training Division.
(Photograph by Masami Onuka)

(Continued from page 70)

The Fifth Day:

Her hair pulls out at the slightest touch of my hand. Maggots clogging suppurating wounds: when poked, they spill and scatter over the floor and then throng back into the pus.

The warehouse where there was not even room to place one's feet for bodies, is now empty except for the helplessly distended remaining victims: they are on the verge of death, squirming in corners as they drive away hovering flies from their wounds, and a few gloomy attendants wait.

The Sixth Day:

A young factory man behind a pillar, only his eyes showing through the bandages swathing his entire body, chants the national anthem faintly and weakly. "There, there, now; just go off to sleep. Call out for Aunty any time and I'll come across to you." A one-eyed woman nearby, bandages covering her head, calls out as she crawls up to him.

"Aunty? You are no Aunty! It's my mother I want, my mother!"

His arms are immobile. He can only turn his face with dark-red cheekbones covered with greasy sweat. Tears trickle down from a glaring pair of eyes beneath the bandages.

The Seventh Day:

Murk in the empty warehouse. In the corner there, a figure sobs interminably, and here by a pillar the last wounded woman, arching in agony, is turning to stone.

The Eighth Day:

The warehouse completely vacant. In the sky through the twisted girders, the smoke ascends from the pyres of the dead heaped up in the vacant lot outside. But the specters remain:

Behind a pillar a quivering hand raises a water-flask:

Multitudinous eyes filled with terror line the bank walls.

Mrs K also has joined the dead.

"Patience: all dead. The names of those deceased are as follows...."

Hiroshima (Late August 1945)
The Danbara Junior High School was used as a relief center.
(Photograph by Army Marine Headquarters)

At the First-Aid Station

Sankichi Toge

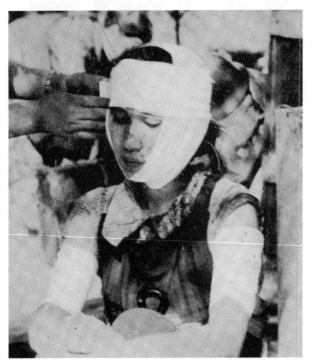

Nagasaki (About 2 p.m., August 10, 1945)
A schoolgirl is undergoing medical treatment with a blank look in her face.
(Photograph by Yosuke Yamahata)

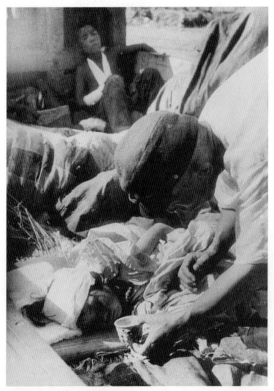

Hiroshima (August 12, 1945)
This little girl does not have even the energy to drink the proffered water.
(Photogra by Hajime Miyatake)

You
Who weep although you have no ducts for tears,
Who cry although you have no lips for words,
Who wish to clasp
Although you have no skin to touch,
You:

Limbs twitching, oozing blood and foul secretions,
Eyes all puffed-up slits of white,
Tatters of underwear
Your only clothing now,
Yet with no thought of shame.
Ah! How fresh and lovely you all were
A flash of time ago
When you were schoolgirls, a flash ago
(Who could believe it now?)

Out from the murky, quivering flames
Of burning, festering Hiroshima
You step (unrecognizable
Even to yourselves),
You leap and crawl, one by one,
Onto this grassy plot,
Wisps of hair on bronze bald heads,
Into the dust of agony.

Why have you had to suffer this?
Why this, the cruelest of afflictions?
Was there some purpose?
Why?
You look so monstrous, but could not know
How far removed you are now from mankind.
You think;
Perhaps you think
Of mothers and fathers, brothers and sisters,
(Could even they know you now?)
Of houses where you slept, waked up and took breakfast.
(The flowers in the hedge scattered in a flash
And even the ashes now have gone.)

Thinking, thinking; you are thinking,
Trapped with friends who ceased to move, one by one,
Thinking when once you were a daughter.
A daughter
Of humanity.

Nagasaki (In the morning of August 10, 1945)
Carrying his little brother on his back,
a boy is looking for their parents.
(Photograph by Yosuke Yamahata)

My Daddy
Keiko Kakita, 3th grade
Honkawa Elementary School, Hiroshima City

Hiroshima, the lively city
My Daddy, who died there
My Daddy, gone, on the cloud of the atomic bomb
My Daddy, who died at the castle
My Daddy, lost when I was little
My Daddy, whose face I don't even know
My Daddy, whose face I would love to see, even once in a dream
My Daddy, I want to call out, and to hold him.
If we did not have a war, my daddy would not have died.
He would have remained in our original home
And the bicycle
Which my big brother wants
Would have been bought.

From *"From under the Atomic Cloud"*

Nagasaki (August 10, 1945)
A municipal officer picks up the arm of a victim to see
her condition. (Photogra by Yosuke Yamahata)

Nagasaki (August 10, 1945)
A woman stands in an state of shock near the hypocenter.
Behind her lies the body of an aged man who could not escape
and burned to death, trapped possibly by the collapse of a house.
(Photograph by Yosuke Yamahata)

This Might Be the Last Time to Give the Breast to My Baby

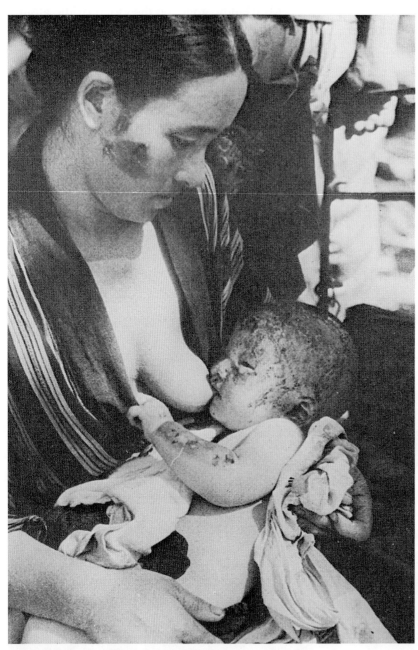

Nagasaki (August 10, 1945)
A mother with her baby in front of the Michinoo Station, 3.5 km from the hypocenter.
(Photograph by Yosuke Yamahata)

My Experience of Atomic Bomb

Toshio Okamoto, 6th grade
Takeya Elementary School,
Hiroshima City

After the atomic bomb,
How many hardships we've gone through!
We had no food.
We ate cakes made from rail-side horseweed.
We wore any kind of clothes.
Burnt-out ruins stretched
To the four corners of Hiroshima.
We returned to the place where we had been before
And waited for our mother to come back.
We went back to our hometown as she didn't come back.
After we went back to our hometown,
I started to receive regular treatment at the clinic of doctor Arase.
One day when I went to the clinic,
The doctor was treating somebody who I didn't know.
When he peeled five or six pieces of skin off the back of the patient, there were thousands of maggots.
I shudder even now when I remember
That terrible atomic bomb.
Don't repeat it again.
Let us live in peace.

From *"From under the Atomic Cloud"*

Grief of Children

Little Child

Sankichi Toge

Little one, my dear,
Where on earth are you now?
Your Mummy has gone from before your wide open eyes;
We were parted on that
Bright clear morning.
It was like suddenly stumbling over a rock.
In the depths of your eyes
Reflecting a spotless sky,
A sudden
Dark reddish cloud reared up
Unfurling itself at the top of heaven,
An unprecedented flash without noise.
Who will explain that day
To your endless innocent questions, my dear?

Little one, my dear,
Where on earth have you gone?
Leaving you in the care of neighbors I went to work.
Later, sustained only by my love for you
I dashed through the burning city
On the rotting flesh of my two feet
Where the maggots had begun to crawl.
But too feeble even to be revolted
Your Mummy died quietly
In the darkness of the first-aid station.

Your Daddy, while I bore you in my womb,
Blown to bits by a shell in a southern island.
Gentle Daddy's body anointed by parting tears,
Swollen with burns, pus and purple blotches,
Writhing under his fellow soldiers.
Leaving only his haversack, unsoiled and unburnt,
(With a new picture book for you) he became still.
Who will tell you of that night?

(Continued on page 76)

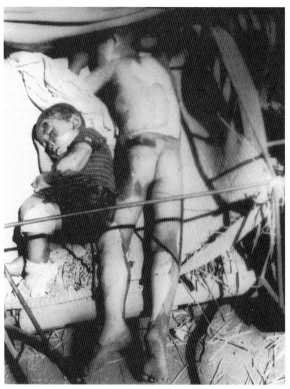

Nagasaki (About 3 p.m., August 10, 1945)
Somebody has brought a boy and a little child by a cart, walking 5 or 6 km from the center of the city. In front of the Michinoo Station.
(Photograph by Yosuke Yamahata)

Nagasaki (In the morning of August 10, 1945)
A boy stands with a rice-ball in hand at Ibinokuchi-machi, 1.8 km south-southeast of the hypocenter.
(Photograph by Yosuke Yamahata)

Hiroshima
"Looking at a baby who was clinging to the breasts of his unconscious mother, I could not hold back my tears."
(Drawn by Kizo Kawakami, aged 40 in 1945.
From "Pictures about the Atomic Bomb Drawn by Citizens")

(Continued from page 75)

Little one, dear,
What on earth are you doing now?
The naked sun quivering beyond the cloud;
Driven by a barrage of sparks and dazzling glass,
Mummy ran straight through the deafened street,
Mummy's fleeing thoughts went like a tremor through the heart.
I screamed out your name, words stumbling.

Only you,
Only you I wanted to tell,
Of your Daddy,
Of your Mummy,
Of the pain I felt as I left you alone.
Who will tell
About this?

That's it!
I will find you,
I will tell you,
Snuggling my lips to your soft ear,
How war severed children from their parents,
How it strangled them slowly with a dark force
Swatted them finally
Like flies;
Gored them to death;
Drove them mad.
How it burned the sea and the islands,
How it burned Hiroshima,
How it wrenched your Daddy,
Snatched your Mummy,
From your clinging hands, from your innocent eyes.
I will tell you
I will tell you the whole truth!

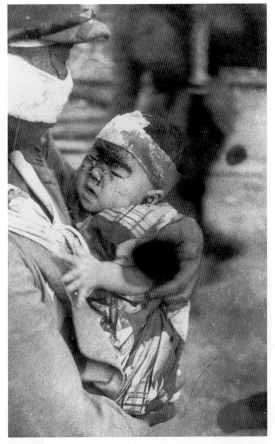

Nagasaki
A man is holding his little son in his arms.
The boy does not have the energy even to cry.
(Photograph by Yosuke Yamahata)

I Would Rather Kill Myself Than Endure Pain of Burns

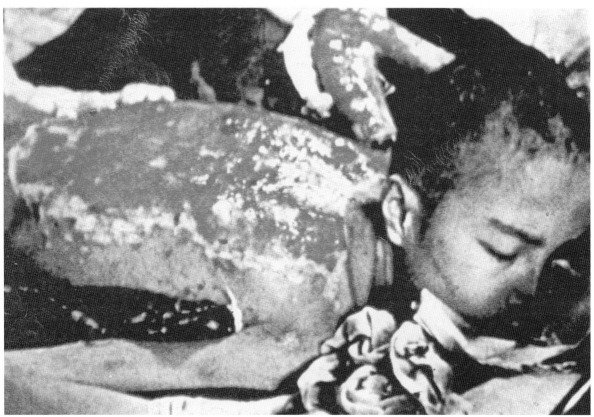

Nagasaki
While delivering telegrams, a 16-years-old postman was exposed to the atomic bomb on the road, 1.8 km from the hypocenter. His entire back was burned out. With excruciating pain, he shouted, "Kill me!"
(Photograph by U.S. Army)

Untitled
Tomoko Sato, 5th grade
Minamikannon Elementary School,
Hiroshima City

Little Yoshiko
In bed
From the burns
Wanted to eat
Tomatoes.
While my Mummy
Was out to buy them
Little Yoshiko died.
My Mummy said
We had only potatoes to give her
And we let her die.
My Mummy cried.
I cried.
Everyone cried.

From *"From under the Atomic Cloud"*

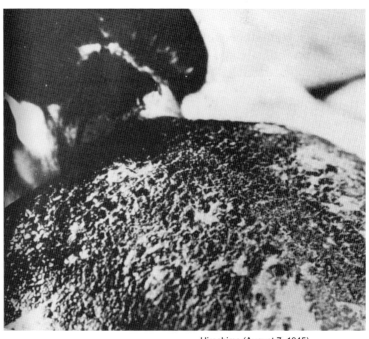

Hiroshima (August 7, 1945)
A woman with thermal burns on her back.
(Photograph by Masami Onuka)

Splinters of Glass Pierced the Whole Body

A man wounded all over his back by broken pieces of glass. (Photograph by Masao Shiotsuki)

Atomic Bomb
Misao Seiki, 6th grade
Takeya Elementary School, Hiroshima City

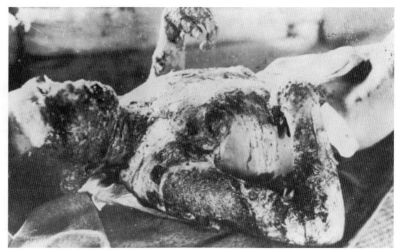

Hiroshima (August 7, 1945) A burnt man. (Photograph by Masami Onuka)

The moment of flash, darkness came.
In a while it got lighter over there.
Looking upward silently, I found myself pinned under stones.
Terrified, I cried,
"Help! Help!"
Then some Uncle called out,
"Where are you? Where are you?"
With his hair disheveled.
I cried for my life, "Here I am!"
The Uncle carried me on his back.
Tottering among stones and crushed houses,
He took me to my home.
In the house there was none found.
Neither of Grandma and Mummy.
Then I heard Mummy calling my name from a distance, "Misao-chan!"
I broke into tears and threw myself into her arms.
She had burns in her face, arms and legs.
"Let's get away from here quickly," saying so to me,
She breathed her last.
I burst out crying.
Since then I have been all alone.
Never should we go to war again.
I don't want another child like me.

From *"From under the Atomic Cloud"*

A Burnt Girl under Treatment

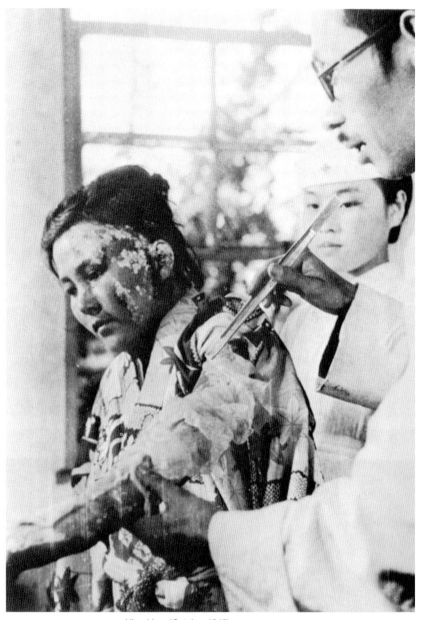

Hiroshima (October 1945)
At the Hiroshima Red Cross Hospital. (Photograph by Shunkichi Kikuchi)

In the case of the burnt people,
Every time the skin was regenerated, it was broken by pus which continued gathering in the wounds.
The pain was so terrible that they would rather kill themselves than endure it.
In such a situation, those who were to die were gone and those who were to survive were left alive.
Seven years after the end of the war
The effects of the atomic bomb still remain.
When the students of the Shinonome-fuzoku Junior High School were asked to write their own personal history,
Nearly all of them touched on the atomic bomb.
This proves how deeply it has infiltrated into the memory of the people of Hiroshima,
How seriously it has injured them through its disease and keloids (excessive growth of scar tissue over a burn).
Some children were too dismayed to remain sane.
Some youths were so shocked that they completely lost their memories.
Some attempted suicide out of despair at their hopeless condition.
Those who could not endure such grief and agony have died during these postwar years.
Those who could, have overcome.
Nevertheless, young girls with keloids in their faces usually stay indoors
Except for August 6, the anniversary of their relatives' death
When they pay a visit to the memorial tower near the hypocenter.
With what could we solace their suppressed tears in their hearts!

Excerpts from *"An Appeal of All Voices"* Sankichi Toge

Innumerable Flies Bred

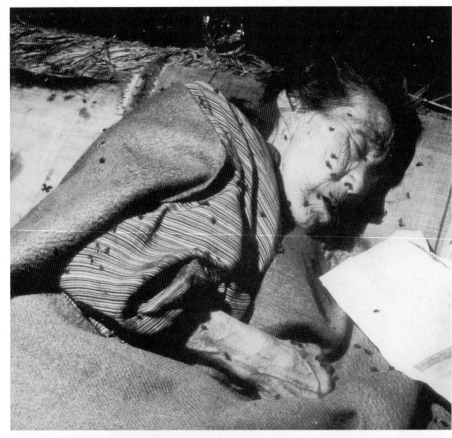

Hiroshima (September 1945)
Maggots get into the wounds and flies swarm over the body of an old woman lying down on the floor. She is left alive only to endure pain in silence.
(Photograph by U.S. Navy)

Hiroshima (September 1945)
Husband and wife in the basement.
(Photograph by U.S. Navy)

Oh, mother! Aged mother!
You can't go like this –.
It is because of your weariness
Searching among the
Burnt-out ruins?
Or it is because of
Lingering poison fumes
That you slump down into
Final sleep?
You mutter away now
But do not understand the words
You mumble, Mother.

Your grief beyond grief
Your grudge beyond grudge
Well up together with the
Hopes and feelings of all
Who have lost their dear ones,
Gathering into a force to ensure
That this tragedy will never
Happen again
In our human world.

So do not die;
You must not leave
Now like this,
Your whispers and dried tears
Etched on your heart trapped
Between shriveled ribs.

Excerpts from *"Aged Mother"*
Sankichi Toge

Symptoms of A-bomb Disease Appeared

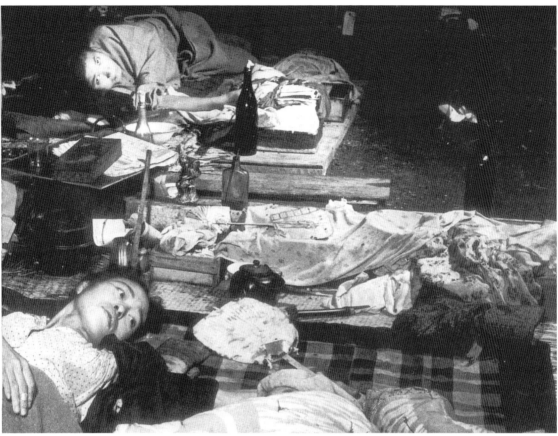

Hiroshima (September 1945) : Most of the A-bomb victims were wounded and lost their homes. One month after that day, some of them were lying down on the straw mats, covered with some blanket-like cloths. The bottles might contain drinking water. The woman at the back stares at the unexpected American photographer. (Photograph by U.S. Navy)

Atomic Bomb
Norie Takahashi, 4th grade
Hirose Elementary School, Hiroshima City

Something flashed.
All of us were trapped under the fallen house.
I was also found under the ruins.
My mother saved me.
I was bleeding at the head.
While fleeing on her back,
I saw burnt and wounded people.
They were groaning with pain.
Hiroshima was
Covered with flames and smoke.
We
Sought refuge in our hometown.
Our dear old home was burned.
Many people were killed.
I'm really afraid of war.
Please never repeat it again.

From *"From under the Atomic Cloud"*

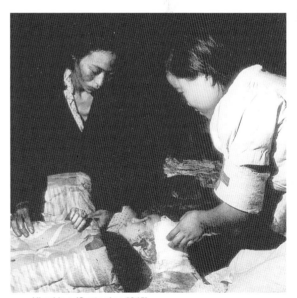

Hiroshima (September 1945)
A photograph of a mother and her daughter taken by an American photographer. They are looking at each other. For what is this girl trying to appeal to her mother with her eyes and mouth? The hands of the nurse show her deep sympathy for the girl. (Photograph by U.S. Navy)

My Head is Bald

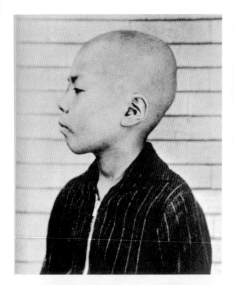
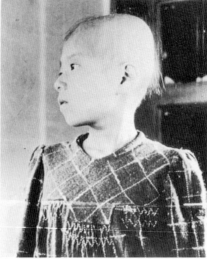

Hiroshima (October 1945)
A girl (right) and her little brother (left) losing their hair. When the atomic bomb detonated, both were doing their homework for the summer peaceably in their house located in Funairi-cho, about 1 km from the hypocenter. Their hair began to fall off in October. The boy died of the A-bomb disease in 1949. The girl grew up, got married and gave birth to a baby, but she also died of the A-bomb after effects in 1965.
(Photograph by Shunkichi Kikuchi and Seiji Saito)

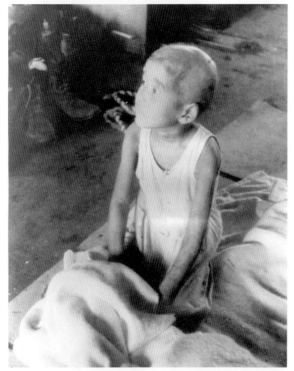

My Head
Kenji Kawai, 4th grade
Funairi Elementary School, Hiroshima City

Pikadon (atomic bomb)
Made me bald.
I felt something wrong also with my eyes.
I was two years old then.

When I grew up
I was called "egg" or "bald."
Also "sore eyes."
I controlled myself.
I felt like crying, but I didn't.

From *"From under the Atomic Cloud"*

Nagasaki (Late August 1945)
A girl losing her hair. Her hair began to fall off in the second week after the bombing and continued for one to two weeks.
(Photograph by Eiichi Matsumoto)

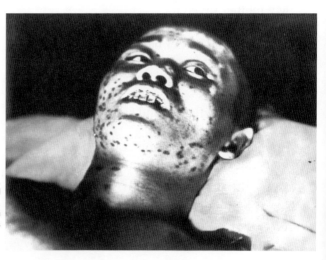

Hiroshima (September 3, 1945)
People were saying,"You are going to die, if spots appear." This soldier was exposed to the atomic bomb at a wooden house, 1 km from the hypocenter. Bleeding from the skin (purple spots), stomatitis and loss of hair were observed.
(Photograph by Gonichi Kimura)

People Die even Without External Wounds

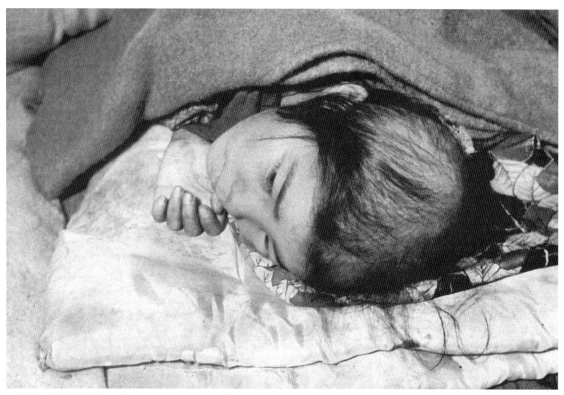

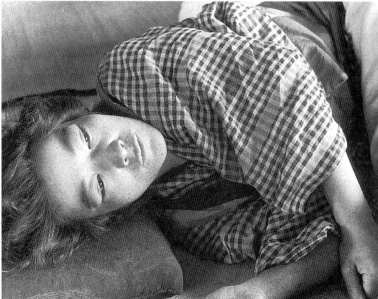

Hiroshima (October 11, 1945)
A girl and her mother at the Oshiba temporary relief center.
(Photographs by Shunkichi Kikuchi)
This little girl, 12 years old, was trapped under a fallen refrigerator and wounded in her right knee and thigh, and the back of her head.
Her mother, 31 years old, suffered no external wounds. She was able to take good care of her daughter. But one month later, symptoms of A-bomb disease appeared like spots, gingival hemorrhage, vomiting and bleeding. Being conscious that these were signs of death, she was sobbing with fear and grief.

As it is described in some poems,
Who could heal the grief of the children called "bald" scornfully?
Even now that seven years have passed since then,
As seen in the case of Hisato Ito, "A-bomb child," who died this spring,
The A-bomb disease is recurring.
Those who have been absolutely fine until now
Are put on the verge of death by a sudden reduction
Or growth of white blood corpuscles.

Excerpts from *"An Appeal of All Voices"* Sankichi Toge

Recurring A-bomb Disease

A woman (right) suffering from microcephaly, a syndrome characterized by an abnormally small head, due to her exposure in the womb of her mother (left).
(At Iwakuni, near Hiroshima, in April 1978)
The exposure to the atomic bomb had a variety of devastating effects on fetuses exposed in their mothers' wombs. Many of them suffered serious mental retardation and/or congenital physical disabilities. They have been able to survive because of their parents' good care.

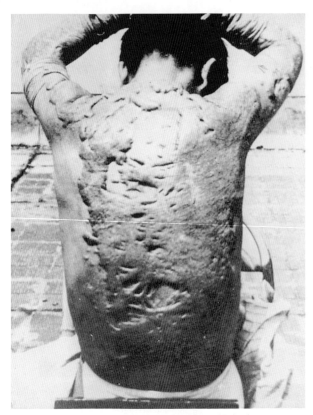

A man with keloids formed on the burnt skin all over his back.
(April 1947, from the American magazine "LIFE")

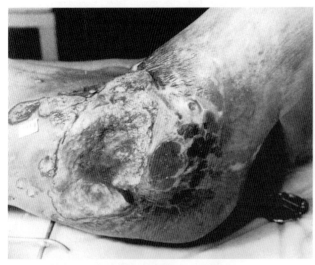

Cancer of the skin in the right buttock of a man who was exposed to the atomic bomb 1.2 km from the hypocenter.
(At the Hiroshima Red Cross Hospital)

> Also the bad genetic effects were pointed out by a scientist (Huxley) and this was published.
> Whatever will happen in the future?
> And if there is no way of treating any of those effects and no prospects of finding new ways in the future,
> Whatever will happen when the atomic attack is repeated again?
> The desperate voices for wishing the atomic bomb not to be used
> And the war not to break out again
> Are raised from this agony.
>
> Excerpts from *"An Appeal of All Voices"*
> Sankichi Toge

A Shadow of the Victim Vanished by the Flash

Hiroshima
Bent steel-frames
of a building.
(850 m from
the hypocenter.
Photograph by
U.S. Army)

Hiroshima (November 20, 1946)
A human shadow imprinted on the steps at the entrance of the Sumitomo Bank at Kamiya-cho, 250 m from the hypocenter. This person must have been sitting on the step with his or her left knee drawn up and right leg stretched. The spot covered the sitting person remained dark, but the surface of the surrounding stone turned white by exposure to the heat rays. The person was vanished by the flash.
(Photograph by Yoshito Matsushige)

Enclosed by a painted fence
In a corner of the bank's stone-steps
A still pattern
In the dark reddish grains of the stone.

On that morning,
An incandescent flash
Burned into the granite plate
Somebody's hips like a shadow.

On the water-red cracked stone steps
The running blood from thickly melting intestines
Still makes a scorched shadow.

Ah, that morning,
Hiroshima people were flung around
Under the incomprehensible
Flash, superheat, and explosive blast,
Swallowed up into the whirls of fire and clouds.
They crawled about dragging their flayed skin
Unrecognizable
Even to their wives and children.
This shadow will forever
Pursue their scarred memories which
Will never effaced.

Excerpts from *"A Shadow"* Sankichi Toge

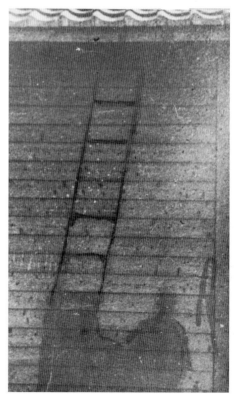

Nagasaki (September 1945)
Shadows imprinted on the wall of the Nagasaki Fortress Headquarters at Minamiyamate-machi, 4.4 km from the hypocenter. A soldier of the air defense personnel was struck by heat rays when he went down from the roof after the air raid alert was lifted. The surface of the tarred wall was burned and the shadows of the soldier and a ladder were imprinted.
(Photograph by Eiichi Matsumoto)

Hiroshima and Nagasaki Turned

Hiroshima (November 1945) : A view from the Kyobashi Bridge, 1.4 km from the hypocenter, toward the center of the city. (Photograph by Yoshito Matsushige)

Nagasaki (October 1945) : A view from a place, 120 m east of the hypocenter. (Photograph by Shigeo Hayashi)

Memories of the Atomic Bomb
Yoshiko Katsuya, 3rd grade
Tsuzumigaura Junior High School, Aki County

At the instant of flash and blast
Hiroshima was destroyed completely.
In deed, in an instant.
That terrific noise
Remains clearly still now in my ears.

Some died.
Others were wounded.
A small number of those survivors
Under the scorching sunshine
Leave Hiroshima to flee for refuge.
With torn clothes, in bare feet
And covered with blood
They look wretched.

Somebody carries the bedding.
Somebody else takes a little child's hand.
Ah, these miserable people,
Where can they sleep tonight?

Children got separated from their mothers.
Mothers got separated from their children.
How sad that when these people met again each
   other at last,

to Rubble and Cinders

Their beloved were already turned into skeletons.
I heard
There was also a pitiful mother
Who lost her mind and died,
As she missed her dead child so much.
The soul of the little child
Who sacrificed its irreplaceable life
And said good-bye to the soil
Should have cursed this unfortunate world.
Poor people,
Pitiful people,
They died in great agony.
All these things happened due to the war.
War – what a hateful word it is!

The most disgraceful thing in the world –
It's a war.
Those who desire a peaceful world
Will surely shout
They absolutely don't want wars any more.

We are advancing
Toward a peaceful world.
Peace, peace
Let us hasten to build peace
By our strength
For our happiness.

From *"From under the Atomic Cloud"*

Blast

The hypocenter due to the rebounding shock waves of the blast.
(Photograph by Toshio Kawamoto)

Hiroshima
A huge 300-years-old camphor tree was blown down by the blast.
(Photograph by Yoshito Matsushige)

Hiroshima
A heavy stone lantern remained tilted because a small stone was caught under it at the moment when it was lifted up by the blast.
(Photograph by Toshio Kawamoto)

Memories of the Atomic Bomb

Kunio Teranishi, 6th grade
Takeya Elementary School, Hiroshima City

My right leg,
Looking at it
I remember what happened that day.
My right leg is so smooth
Quite different from other parts of my body
Because it was burned and skinned that day.
This wound will not heal probably forever.
Whenever I look at this wound
I feel distress.
I see those who writhed in agony and died in my mind's eye.
I shudder at these memories.
The war should never be repeated.

From *"From under the Atomic Cloud"*

Why was the Atomic Bomb Used?

It was a well-designed surprise raid on a city congested with unarmed civilians

Introduction to the collection of poems
"From under the Atomic Cloud" (Summary)
By Sankichi Toge on August 3 1952

In the Yalta Conference, held on February 1945, it was agreed that in three months after Germany had surrendered, the Soviet Union should enter into the war against Japan. On April 1, U.S. forces landed in Okinawa. On April 5, Soviet Foreign Minister Molotov notified Japan that the Soviet Union would not renew the Japanese-Soviet Non - Aggression Pact.

On May 8, Germany proclaimed its unconditional surrender. The U.S. and the Great Britain pushed forward with the landing operation at Normandy with the aim of getting Berlin earlier than the Soviet Union which turned to a counterattack at Stalingrad although the former had delayed opening up a second front in Europe. While in Asia,the Japanese people could not know that the U.S. also aimed to break in and use the Japanese military power against next opponents.

While forcing the people to prepare for the decisive battle in the mainland, the Japanese financial and military ruling groups designated the representative of the Yokohama Bank in Switzerland to negotiate with the U.S. business group with the aim of finding opportunities to end the war and preserve the Emperor system.

On June 21, the Japanese armed forces ended their organized resistance in Okinawa. On July 16, the first atomic bomb explosion in the world was conducted in New Mexico. The Potsdam Conference was held the next day and its declaration was published on July 26. It was already apparent that the Soviet Union would declare war against Japan on August 8. It was also easily expected how fast the Soviet armed forces would smash the Japanese counterparts.

The process becomes more evident if I quote Mr. Paul Nitze, Vice Chairman of the U.S. Strategic Bombing Survey, who stated, "The swift bombing on Hiroshima and Nagasaki was a brilliant success in a sense that its political purpose was fully achieved. The U.S. control over Japan is perfect so that there cannot be room for Russia to scramble for the power in Japan."

Then the whole city of Hiroshima burst into flames. Innumerable people died looking for water and groaning with pain. But munitions plants like Mitsubishi Shipbuilding, Mitsubishi Heavy Industry, Asahi Armament, Nihon Steel, Toyo Industry, etc. were hardly damaged. The National Railways lines were restored within three days.

On August 9, when the Soviet tanks were advancing to attack the Japanese army in China, the second atomic bomb was dropped on Nagasaki.

On August 14, Japan accepted the Potsdam Declaration and the Emperor issued his message to declare the end of the war the following day. The Emperor and the military intended to shift the reason for having lost the war to the atomic bombs. But no sooner had they surrendered than they began to propagate the absolute power of the atomic bomb. "Chugoku Shinbun" dated August 15 wrote, "The destructive power of this bomb is as big as 20,000 tons of TNT" "Mainichi Shinbun" dated August 24 wrote, "The atom-bombed place will be uninhabitable for 70 years." This kind of propaganda was taken over by the U.S. forces which occupied Japan. In the meantime, those citizens who could have survived were suffering from loss of hair, fever, diarrhea, vomiting and internal bleeding and died one after another by the end of 1945.

The citizens of Hiroshima who were in such a horrible situation had to endure a daily hard life. Dr. K.T. Compton said, "The use of the atomic bomb would have saved hundreds of thousands, probably millions of lives of Americans and Japanese " The fact that Hiroshima of Jodo Shinshu Buddhism and Nagasaki of Catholicism had been chosen as targets of the atomic bombing made the deceptive propaganda more effective.

Atomic Bombs

Atomic bombs

When a single free neutron strikes the nucleus of an atom of fissile material like uranium 235 or plutonium 239, it splits the nucleus and usually knocks two or three more neutrons free. Enormous energy (intense heat, blast and lethal radiation) is released when those neutrons split off from the nucleus. The newly released neutrons strike other nuclei, splitting them in the same way and releasing more energy and neutrons. Under certain conditions, this fission process can spread in an instant and trigger a chain reaction that generates tremendous power. The atomic bomb is a weapon of mass slaughter that uses this tremendous power released instantaneously by the splitting of atomic nuclei.

Manhattan Project

When World War II broke out in 1939, U.S. President Roosevelt ordered that the atomic bomb development project should be started. The "Manhattan Project" was launched in August 1942 to produce an atomic bomb. It was carried out in extreme secrecy with a large sum of the national budget by a great number of scientists.

		Hiroshima	Nagasaki
Type		Gun barrel type A-bomb "Little Boy"	Implosion type A-bomb "Fat Man"
	Weight	Approx. 4 tons	Approx. 4.5 tons
	Destructive power	Approx. 15,000 tons of TNT	Approx. 21,000 tons of TNT
	Height of explosion	580±15 m	500±10 m
	Structure	Uranium 235 was divided into two parts, both of which were below a critical mass, and placed at either end of a cylinder. An explosive device was used to slam one portion of uranium to the other, instantly creating a critical mass and causing nuclear fission. As natural uranium contains a very low percentage of uranium 235, the development of a special technique was essential for separation of uranium 235 from natural uranium.	Plutonium 239 was divided into subcritical portions and packed into a spherical case. Gunpowder around the periphery of the case was touched off to force the portions to the center and increase the density of the plutonium, instantly creating a critical mass and causing nuclear fission. As plutonium 239 does not exist in the natural world, the development of a nuclear reactor was indispensable for its production.

Atomic Bomb Damage

	Hiroshima	Nagasaki
Time of explosion	08:15 a. m. August 6, 1945	11:02 a. m. August 9, 1945
Deaths and missing persons (population before A-bombings)	Approx. 140,000 (±10,000) Approx. 350,000	Approx. 74,000 (±10,000) Approx. 240,000
Damage to buildings (number before A-bombings)	Approx. 76,000	Approx. 51,000
Complete destruction and burning	63%	23%.
Complete destruction	5%	2%
Half destruction, burning or significant damage	24%	11%
Total	92%	36%

A-bomb "Little Boy" on Hiroshima

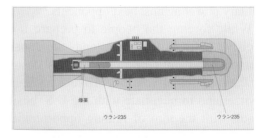

A-bomb "Fat Man" on Nagasaki

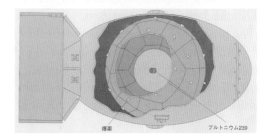

Atomic Bomb Damage

The atomic bomb is a weapon which uses enormous energy released by the nuclear fission to cause a vastly increased magnitude of instantaneous and mass destruction and slaughter. The released energy turns into heat rays, blast and radiation which act synergistically to generate a huge destructive power. The urban districts of Hiroshima and Nagasaki were utterly destroyed. Radiation damage continues to this day to injure the health of the survivors who live in fear, wondering when its aftereffects might appear.

The acute effects subsided in four to five months, but five to six years after the bombing, an increase in leukemia and other aftereffects emerged as a serious problem. The aftereffects included keloids (mounds of scar tissue swelling over healed burns), cataract, leukemia, thyroid cancer, breast cancer, lung cancer and various other cancers, as well as microcephaly, a syndrome characterized by mental and physical retardation that struck in-utero survivors.

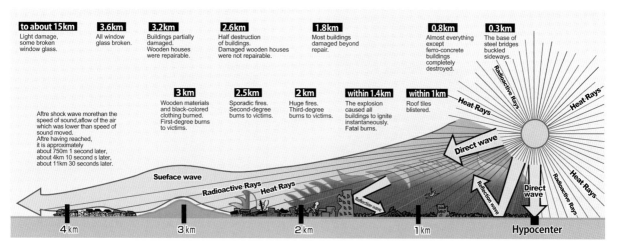

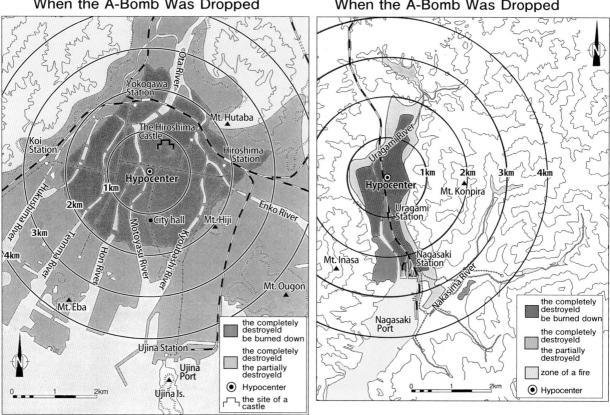

The Hiroshima City Map at the Time When the A-Bomb Was Dropped

The Nagasaki City Map at the Time When the A-Bomb Was Dropped

A Gravepost

Sankichi Toge

You all stand huddled together,
Like a children's hustle-jostle on a winter day,
Squeezed and pushed into a corner of the town.
Now
You are just one small gravepost
Nobody will notice.

"In memory of Seibi Primary School War Victims."

Enclosed on a base of burnt bricks

Nagasaki (October 1945)
Pupils of the Shiroyama Elementary School were reduced to bleached bones.

A piece of wood less than three feet high stands,
A bamboo flower tube leans now cracked and flowerless.

Behind "A. B. Advertising Company"
"C. D. Scooter Commercial Enterprises"
And a colossal hoarding saying
"Hiroshima Peace Metropolitan Construction Company,"
The backs of these lined up plated buildings, painted green,
At the corner of the alley
Leading through to MacArthur Trophy Tennis Courts,

Piles of discarded tiles and cement waste,
The fallen school gate half-buried
Where muddy water gathers on a rainy day,
Dilapidated municipal dwellings – shanties
Where the ceaseless wailing of babies is heard,

Here you stand,
A decaying wooden post
Without hands,
Without feet,
With no one to coax
Or pester for things,
Without words, without voices,
You stand.

No matter how much you call
No matter how much you cry
Your Daddies and Mummies
Will never come.
Wrenching off your clinging hands perhaps
The adults left, fleeing from you
As you were pressed under a heavy heap of rubble
In hot scorching wind
Stuck in a dark choking space.
(What terrible mischief had you done....?)
Your soft hands,
Your young necks,
How easily they were crushed
And squeezed of blood,
Ground under stones, steel and old timber.

In the shadow of Mt. Hiji
A line of friends, their eyes like burnt buns,
Crouching down not knowing what to do,
At the clatter of the running soldiers' side-arms,
Cried, "Soldier, help me!"
But nobody acknowledged them,
By the darkening water-tank,
Even when they pointed west saying,
"Take me with you!"
Nobody took their hands.

Then like the others they got into the water-tank,
Covering their faces with fig leaves,
And died,
All of them,
Without understanding.

You cannot smell the apples,
You cannot taste the lollipops,
You have gone to a far off place.

(Continued on page 95)

(Continued from page 94)
Who made you say,
"I want nothing until victory"?
"In memory of Seibi Primary School War
Victims."

The bewildered look in your eyes:
You stand here silently watching —
The abandoned field gun your brothers and fathers were
Forced to cling to, rusting red;
A foreign soldier and a Japanese girl
Lying in a clover-patched dip,
Observed from your corner,
And
Again today, war protesters led
To the detention center
Surrounded by a high new wall in the field
Across the way from your corner.

How strange it all is!
Your ears, keen as a rabbit's, hearing
The raucous radio elatedly blurting out
From beneath the eaves of the thin wooden roof
How many hundred tons of bombs were dropped,
By how many millions of dollars
The budget for the manufacture
Of atomic weapons has been increased
And how reinforcements will land in Korea.*
Even rusty nails are gathered
From beneath the roots of the grassy-smelling horseweed,
And sold for the war.
Ah, you will be gathered up
And forgotten
A solitary sign-post barely remains
But it will soon be buried by land-developers.
This place where the small bones of your hands
And your neck bones are buried
Will be covered in buildings
And be seen no more.

"In memory of Seibi Primary School War Victims."

Although there are no flowers in the flower tube,
Two butterflies flit around chasing each other,
The breeze from the sea
Touches the weather-worn grain of the post,
And the sky is bright blue
As on that morning.

Won't you come out, little ones?
Linking soft arm in soft arm
Won't you rise from here?

Your granny
Is waiting for you even now.
Saying, "Is there anyone who will go to the Peace Festival
As though it were a gala?"
Under the rose bush
Granddad has secretly hidden your old shoes.

The babies who survived that day
Sucking at the breasts of their dead mothers,

Hiroshima (December 1947)
For the A-bomb orphans, an easy way of earning money was the shining of shoes on the street. These shoeshine boys gathered spontaneously in front of the Hiroshima Railway Station or on the busy streets.

Are now six.
Your friends
Who loitered on the rainy streets
Stealing and begging
Are now deep-tanned, brawny and sinewy
As grown-ups.
"We won't lose,
We'll win,"
Say your Korean friends
At Hiroshima Station under the glaring sun,
Collecting signatures opposing the war.
"We won't lose,
We'll win,"
Say the Japanese children
Discarding their shoeshine brushes
To sell a newspaper telling the truth.

Little ones,
Do not be silent. Speak up,
To fight against the adults all over the world
Who are trying to bring about war.
Spring out shouting "Hey!"
With loud clear voices,
Your round eyes shining;
And open your arms
(Free to hug everyone),
Give an embrace that will bring back
Tears of good to everyone's heart.
Then spring at them all over the world
Shouting, "We are the boys and girls,
The Children of Hiroshima!"

Appealing
Sankichi Toge

Even now it's not too late;
Still it's not too late to muster your true
    power
If you have tears which fall unceasingly
(Your heart pierced by the flash
That scorched your eyes that day)
Or if you still reek
Of Hiroshima where the curse of war
Drips in bloody pus from the wounds.

It's not too late for you
Who abandoned your sister squirming,
Both her arms thrust out
From beneath the flame-enveloped
    house,
And staggered off on a bitter journey
Through a desert of glaring rubble,
Not even covering your private parts
    with bits of charred cloth,
Tottering on feet burnt bare,
Red skinless arms dangling across your
    breast.

It's not too late even now for you
To hold up the cursed sun which is
About to drop again –
By thrusting your crippled arms out
    high

With throngs of arms like
    yours,
With your back bearing the
    brand of death
Drying the tears of all those
    gentle people
Who, although they hate
    war, just stand still.
Let them grasp each other
    firmly
With those timid limp hands;
Let them grasp your red
    peeled palms.
Even now,
It's not too late.

The A-bomb Dome
 (Former Hiroshima Prefectural Industrial Promotion Hall)
viewed from the hypocenter.

Young people from Yamaguchi Prefecture and member of the A-bomb Survivors' Association
of Shimonoseki participated in the "Hiroshima Peace Tour" and recited jointly the Toge's poem
"August 6th" in front of the monument dedicated to him. (August 6, 2000)

Defeat – the War Ended at Last

Why were as many as 3.2 million people killed?

U.S. Occupied

"Emperor is equivalent to one million troops"
(Douglas MacArthur)

MacArthur and headquarters staff arrived in Atsugi, Japan. (August 30, 1945)

We will hold the military authorities responsible for the war and use the Emperor as a puppet.

"Japan Plan"   (Occupation plan of the U.S. which was made soon after the attack on Pearl Harbor)

"We will use the Japan Emperor as a symbol of peace without giving the name carefully."

"To point out the lack of legitimacy of today's military authorities government and the fact that this government imperiled the entire Japan including the Emperor and the Imperial Family."

Seized rifles being transported under surveillance of the occupation army.

Memorandum of Reischauer
(U.S. secret service OSS personnel agent at that time)

"After winning the U.S. - Japanese War, we will make a puppet government led by Hirohito."

"We transmit tenaciously correct and intellectual information to 500 Japanese leaders who are permitted to listen to the shortwave broadcasting."

Japan Exclusively

We planned to dispatch 1 million armed forces to Japan, but the dispatch of 250,000 was really enough. Proposal to MacArthur by Brigadier General Fellers who was engaged in Psychological Operation towards Japan.

"We required the help of the Emperor for performing a bloodless invasion. 7 million Japanese soldiers abandoned weapons, and mobilization is stopped immediately by an order of the Emperor. Hundreds of thousands of American casualties were avoided by the measures of the Emperor, and the war terminated earlier than as planned."

"If the Emperor is hung in the court on the charge of war crimes, the ruling mechanism will collapse, and nationwide revolt will not be avoided. Even if they are disarmed, the Japanese soldiers will have confusion and it will be a bloody disaster. With tens of thousands of civil affairs executives, we will need a large-scale dispatch forces."

The signing ceremony of the capitulation was held on the battleship U.S. Missouri.

The true nature of the aggression rule of the U.S. on Japan

"Germany and Italy surrendered, and, at the stage when the defeat of Japanese imperialism became extremely clear, the U.S. repeated indiscriminate bombing on the Japanese mainland and dropped A-bombs on Hiroshima and Nagasaki. The purpose was to put Japan under their control, and by using force to oppress the Japanese people who would rise into action against the Imperial-system of government. Therefore, at the stage when the defeat of the Japanese imperialism became decisive, the U.S. imperialism hastened its landing in Japan."

"They took up power from the hand of the Absolute Emperor System. They took up a special privilege of the absolutism from the Emperor, the privileged bureaucrat and the armed faction, took up a political voice, and confiscated property. They retained the Emperor for his figure and gave a salary of 3,000,000-4,000,000 yen a year through the Diet and did it in "a symbol" to follow the Constitution. The purpose is to hide that U.S. imperialism became the new ruler, and to make use of the Emperor and his close aides for the rule of U.S. in Japan. Therefore, the U.S. did not subject the Emperor on a Far East trial and oppressed the people's struggle against the Emperor system."

From the pamphlet *"How do you look at the modern Japan?"* written by Masayoshi Fukuda, in 1969

Konoe reported to the Emperor (February 14, 1945)

"The defeat is regrettably inevitable. The following report is based on this premise.

The defeat is a serious affair, but the British and American public opinion does not extend to the change of the national polity. Therefore, it is not necessary to worry about defeat if the national polity does not result to a change. The most anxious outcome in maintaining the national polity is communist revolution as a result of the defeat. I think that the internal and external situation is progressing towards communist revolution rapidly."

(Konoe was a closed aide to the Emperor.)

War Took Our Parents, Brothers and Sisters' Lives and People Were Left in a Devastated Situation

3.2 million people were killed in total and household goods were burned.

"Food shortage became more unbearable after the war."

People were boarding a train bound for the countryside to buy food.

Shanties built in a fire-devastated area.

Distribution of sweet potatoes under ration system just after the war.

"Major General Moran's Instruction"
(stayed in Nagoya)

"As successful measures of Japan Occupation by the Coalition Forces, first was to take advantage of food supply shortage, for a while, and total blockade of all food supplies should be done. The first target is to weaken the resistance power of the Japanese people. This target should be done as the top priority. Next target is to destroy their militarism. At the stage of accomplishment of disarmament, then measures used would be like this; increase gradually the amount of surplus foods imported from U.S. Next step is to give the Japanese our hands and support them through economic aids with or without compensation. Such procedures would make the Japanese people think, "U.S. saved us". Until this condition would be prevailed, never give permission to the Japanese government to increase the amount of food supply, even if the amount of production of rice and wheat has increased domestically."

(From the book *"War Story in Nagoya"* ritten by Kaoru Nakanishi)

Emperor, Business Circles, Bureaucrats and Politicians Pretended to Be Pacifists Just As the War Ended

MacArthur and Emperor.

"Despite the so-called Emperor's memo which shows Emperor's disapproval to the top-ranking war leaders, I can't help feeling that the Emperor was so irresponsible. Many people were sent to the front under the order of the Emperor and those who fought for the sake of the Emperor and their fatherland, I must say, died in vain. I wonder why he didn't oppose the war at the court before Japan's entry into WWII or announce the end of war before the dropping of the atomic bomb on Hiroshima." (A war-worn veteran, Shimonoseki)

Japanese financial circles welcomed the surrender to the U.S. and their occupation even said ; "Our time has come."

"Japan's defeat in the WWII has a bright side:people can work at their wills. Free trade with foreign countries, which was restricted during war time, will make the rebuilding of Japan possible." (Iwasaki Koyata, Leader of Mitubishi Zaibatsu)

Prince and his American private teacher.

"Hearing the news of the end of the war, both Yoshisuke Ayukawa and Ryouzou Asano looked completely happy. Being a corporate business between U.S. and Japan. Having studied in America when he was young, Asano had a lot of American acquaintances including President Theodore Roosevelt. Besides, a lot of people cracked open bottles of champagne to celebrate the beginning of a new era."

(From "My Autobiography" by Aiichiro Fujiyama)

Tokyo Trial acquitted the Emperor of the charge and held Hideki Tojo and other military leaders responsible for the war.

The Leadership of the Communist Party Considered the U.S. to Be a Democratic Force

Kyuichi Tokuda, Shigenori Kuroki, Yoshio Shiga – leaders of the Communist Party were released from the Fuchu prison, Tokyo. (October 10, 1945)

"All mobile means have come except for tanks."
– The U.S. occupation army got involved directly in suppressing the employees of Toho movie production company who occupied their workshops in their fight against dismissal of 270 employees.

Compulsory delivery of new rice under U.S. occupation.
Armed MPs of the occupation army forced Japanese farmers to deliver their rice to the government.

The leadership of the Communist Party thanked the U.S. occupation army

From "Appeal to the People"

"The beginning of the democratic revolution in Japan was opened by the stationing of the Alliance Armed Forces for world liberation from fascism and militarism in Japan. We express our will of deep thanks for this.

We support positively the peaceful policy of U.S., Britain and the allied powers armed forces."

October 10, 1945
Comrades of the Japanese Communist Party released from the prison
  Kyuichi Tokuda, Yoshio Shiga
  and other members.

The Japanese Communist Party considered U.S. forces as "a liberation army"

Japanese Communist Party rebuilt after the war split in 1950 because it defined the U.S. occupation forces as a liberation army.

When many Japanese citizens revolted against the Japanese government or Bourgeoisie, the U.S. occupation forces suppressed them. For example, the strike that Government and Public Workers Union's workers carried out nationwide strike in February 1947 was suppressed by Macarthur. After that, the U.S. occupation forces suppressed the workers who carried out strikes throughout the country. As mentioned before, the U.S. occupation forces suppressed the peasants who resisted delivering things to the government.

In this way, the U.S. occupation forces helped the Bourgeoisie and reorganized Japan strongly as they planned on using the government of Japan and local government.

They thought this is wrong. So they thought they need to discuss about the problem of the atomic bomb. The Chugoku regional committee in the center uncovered about the atomic bomb and they started a protest about it in the end of 1949 to the beginning of 1950.

(Masayoshi Fukuda "Along with several ten million public")

Japan Became a Dependency of the U.S.

U.S. suppressed Japanese people by pretending to be a democratic force

"The U.S. occupation forces came to Japan pretending to make Japan a democratic country, but what they actually did was to suppress Japan's working class, urban labor, peasants, medium and small Bourgeoisie, while, protecting and bringing up the monopolistic Bourgeoisie. They made the monopoly Bourgeoisie favorable and obedient to America. They succeeded in making it the ruler of Japan in a relatively short time from 1945 to 1950. While making Japan a subordinate country to America, on the other hand, they used Japan as a base and started the Korean invasion war in 1950. The Japanese monopolistic Bourgeoisie was involved in this war aggressively, earning a lot of dollars from the Korean's blood and got wealth (became rich)."

(Masayoshi Fukuda "Along with several ten million public")

The Emperor made a round of visits throughout the country, always being guarded by the U.S. occupation army.

The truth of rebuilding Japan after the War

"They (America) said they will disassemble the powerful zaibatsu which is dominating Japan. However, they deceived it. First, they put pressure on the monopoly Bourgeoisies who surrendered to American imperialism. Next, they disassembled the homologism to some extent that features the Japanese zaibatsu and made a group of Japanese companies that America can invest to them freely. Finally, they subordinated the monopoly Bourgeoisies and made them ally's to America. They pressured and dominated Japanese citizens by this system.

They made peasants to buy the landlord's land as part of "agricultural land reform". This is not as exactly as to release farmers from the land that they were restricted. American empire thought that existence of landlord was a obstacle to dominate, invest Japan and exploit from Japanese citizens. They needed to exploit the farmers directly. They wanted to exploit from the monopoly Bourgeoisies directly in the end. The fact that the population of agriculture decreased to one third in a short time indicates that."

(Masayoshi Fukuda "How to see the modern Japanese")

A mass rally for an overall peace treaty.

A U.S. mission proposed to the Japanese government that "educational reforms" be carried out.

"Both German Hitler and Italian Mussolini have died. The U.S. kept only the Japanese Emperor alive and used him. The U.S. performed the dissolution of the zaibatsu (big financial group), agrarian reform and the women's right to vote, but all of them were tactics for ruling over Japan. The dissolution of the zaibatsu only changed the financial group into pro - U.S. and only made things more convenient for the U.S."

(Mutsuo Utsunomiya, Oita prefecture)

The Citizen's Disgrace under U.S. Occupation

Shimonoseki occupation of occupation force. (September. 1945)

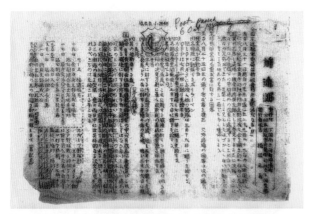

Organ "Zenshin" №3. (Issue person in charge Fukuda Masayoshi)

"The so-called occupation forces came to Shinko. First is. American Marine Corps. Next is. Australians. And last is, New Zealanders. They had stolen the canned meat and potatoes, cigarettes or chocolates from the warehouses and sold them for the money to drink. On the day of inventory, they set fire to the warehouse so that their thieves would not come out. Similar fires broke out a few times. Several factories were also set fire."

(Eiji Yamamoto, former employee of Shinko)

"One night, a fire engine was mounting a hill. At that moment, an automobile driven by an American rushed down toward the fire engine. The driver of the engine was dazzled and his engine spun three times and dropped off the slope. The driver died on the spot. For all, the American driver was to blame."

(Yasunori Murakami, former fire fighter)

The First Strike by Japanese Laborers Against the U.S. Armed Forces

In January,1947, GHQ occupied Yamaguchi Prefecture and the U.S. armed forces entered the Chofu Factory of Kobe Seiko in Shimonoseki. Some of the American soldiers were so vulgar that they put the double XX mark on the walls of Japanese houses if their demands for women were denied.

The U.S. forces were so oppressive that the Japanese workers organized a labor union. Masayoshi Fukuda the union leader, started to plot a strike against the Americans. One morning, a labor rally was held on the playground of Toyoura Senior High School.

Fukuda made a speech to the workers and said he was going to Chofu to negotiate and come with him if they please. So many followed him to Shimonoseki employment bureau. When he was making a speech on a table and starting to negotiate, someone tried to arrest him, showing an arrest warrant signed by the Occupation Forces. Fukuda could not help but go with the person in his automobile. To his surprise, however, many Japanese laborers were waiting in Chofu to rescue Fukuda. His followers were planting themselves in the path of the American automobile. Thanks to his followers, Fukuda was finally freed. Nobody revealed to the U.S. Forces the name of the leader of their union, Fukuda later said.

There Was No End of War for the U.S.

U.S. went to wars incessantly in China, Korea and Vietnam, by using Japan as its base

Then U.S. Secretary of State Dulles made an inspection of 38th parallel north during Korean War.

"During the war, I was captured and held in an American internment camp. At that time I was under an assumed name and kept it secret that I was a combat pilot. But one day Japanese-American came and told me that they knew I was a pilot and suggested that I should cooperate with American Force during the conflict in China and Korea. I as well as other Japanese captive soldiers firmly rejected that kind of offer. We finally came back home in January of 1946. I still believe that we took right decisions." (Kenji Yasuoka, Shimonoseki)

Make use of Unit 731
"Brief Summary of New Information about Japanese B.W. Activities" from Norbert H. Fell's report

In Fell's report made in December 12, 1947 he wrote as follows. "If we get the data of human experimentation connected with the data of ours and the Allied Powers, it will be clear that those data is very valuable. The information about pathological research and human sickness may be very useful in our attempts to develop effective vaccine for anthrax and the plague. As we can completely understand about the bacteriological research of Japan now, there is a good chance to get the useful information about their results in the field of chemical warfare, a death ray and the study of the navy."

A U.S. warplane takes off from a base in Iwakuni, Japan to participate in Korean War.

Then U.S. Secretary of Defense McNamara visits a front line in Vietnam War.

The Occupation Force Concealed the Truth of World War II by Establishing a more Severe Censorship System than the Japanese System during the War

A workshop of censors under the General Headquarters (GHQ) of the occupation force.

A page censored by the occupation force. It is the first page of an article written by historian Kiyoshi Inoue, which was supposed to be carried in the magazine "My University." A paragraph about starvation was deleted.

The U.S. did not permit the use of the symbol used in place of censored words

"After the war, we were tormented for sly censorship." "The postwar censorship was more terrible than the wartime censorship of Japan. The U.S. did not allow to write certain things and several lines were deleted."

(From the book *"My Life and Literature"* written by Shigeharu Nakano)

"There were more than 6000 examiners of the CCD (censorship organization of the GHQ) in the entire country during the golden age. Most of them were Japanese who could understand English. They translated or summarized suspicious sentences and submitted it to the boss. During the four years when CCD was active, 330 million mails were inspected. As for the telephone, approximately 800,000 personal calls were intercepted."

(From the book *"Embracing Defeat"* written by John W. Dower)

"While the notorious Japanese Ministry of Home Affairs censored publications using an apparent way, like placing asterisk like "xxxx", GHQ covered the fact of the censorship itself in an ingenious manner."

(From the book "*The Historical Materials of Yamaguchi Prefecture, ModernIII*" written by Hiroshi Onishi)

Hardship of Life in the Ruins of War

"Finally the war ended, but our situation was as poor as ever. We had relied on the ration system for such foods as rice and sugar. We had been given coupons for clothing. My family were farmers, so some people from Toatsu visited us with their girdles or kimono to barter for crops. Mitsubishi Shipyard gave its workers a special leave to go shopping. Many people walked to Kawatana or Yasuoka to get supplies."

(A clothing store owner, Hikoshima)

Tanaka-machi, Shimonoseki-shi. (1946)

People went to a producing district to buy food.

"After the war, many merchant ships sunk by touching the mines dropped by the US forces along the Kanmon channel.

Along with the ships, many people were sacrificed. We swam to the stranded ships to collect rice or cotton. Those bitter days are still lurking in my heart."

(Jiro Masumoto, Mimosusogawa)

"Five days after the Shimonoseki Air Attack, I gave birth to a baby in an air-raid shelter in Inariyama, Okukoji. Unexpectedly, a midwife happened to be in the same shelter. She was a great help to me. I made diapers by cutting kimono which I had gotten from my aunt in Kokura. It was not easy to find baby goods after the air-raid.

My other child born after the war died of amebic dysentery when she was three years old. My daughter who was born in the air-raid shelter is still fragile because of nutrition deficiency in my womb. Without that formidable war, there would have been no air-raids and children would not have died."

(Michiko Tanaka, Sonoda)

People returned from Manchuria soon after the war.

From Painful Ruination

Hiroshima (October 15, 1945) : Shacks built near the Yokogawa Station. (Photograph by Shunkichi Kikuchi)

Nagasaki (September 1945) : Girls going back home, carrying the distributed food on their shoulders. (Photograph by Eiichi Matsumoto)

We Became Poor
Masazumi Endou, 6th grade
Takeya Elementary School, Hiroshima City

My little sister Yoshie died during the war.
She always ate soybeans because we had no rice.
She suffered always from diarrhea
And died at last.
Soon after that
The atomic bomb was dropped.
I fled with my mother.
All our relatives died.
Recently
My mother often says
She feels lonely.
One hundred thousand lives
Were lost
In an instant.
All people of Hiroshima
Became poor
Like beggars.
And still now
We live in poverty.

From *"From under the Atomic Cloud"*

"You Loitered on the Rainy Streets, Stealing and Begging."

Hiroshima: Children playing around the A-bomb Dome. (Photograph by Yuichiro Sasaki)

A-bomb orphans at war casualty children's homes. In the case of a class at an elementary school within 1 km from the hypocenter, one third of the 60 pupils lost their parents to the A-bomb. About 500 orphans were accommodated at 5 homes in Hiroshima. But there were many who escaped from the homes and ended up living on the street.

Hardships of "A-bomb Widows"

Hiroshima
Many women worked as day laborers in construction sites. Among them were "A-bomb widows" and those young women who could not find other jobs due to keloids in their faces.

Atomic Bomb

Suzuko Yamashiro, 2nd grade
Futaba Junior High School, Hiroshima City

I was seven and my little sister
   was three.
Our father should be fighting the
   war somewhere in northern
   China.
We had received no news from
   him for a very long time.

That day,
Our mother went downtown
For a voluntary work
To clear up the debris of evacuat-
   ed houses.

I was learning with my friends
At a hall near my house.

8:15 a.m.,
At that moment
The atomic bomb was dropped
   on us,
Full of beautiful lights and
   shines.
Treading windowpanes scattered
   on the floor.
I ran away and went back home.
Because I felt that something
   horrible was following me.
I missed my mother so much
And loved her to fold me to her
   breast.
At home,
I found my sisters
Embracing each other
On the tatami mat covered with
   dust
Under the bent ceiling.

Two hours later,
Burnt over her whole body
Breathing very feebly
Our mother – the only one moth-
   er of ours,
The pillar of our family, as our
father was abroad – came back.

My big sister
Brewed Dokudami herb tea
   everyday for our mother
Put face powder on her wound at
   the root of two fingers,
After taking off the scab and
   clearing maggots from the
   wound.

During these seven years
Many things have happened.
I am thirteen and my little sister
   is nine.
Our father did not come back. He
   was killed in the war.

Our mother,
Crippled by that atomic bomb,
Hoes the field
Also today.

From *"From under the Atomic Cloud"*

Are the A-bomb Survivors Guinea Pigs?

"They examined us, but didn't give us any medical treatment." The Atomic Bomb Casualty Commission (ABCC) was set up by the U.S. Forces just to follow and investigate the effects of the bomb on the human body and gather data. They called survivors to the site, stripped girls to the skin and examined even newly-born babies.

I wonder then if you thought
Of your childhood sunflowers along the dike,
A fragrant kimono (Japanese traditional clothes)
  collar mother wore once a year,
Your sister's wheedling after the war had
  worsened,
The lip-stick you put on and rubbed off
With a friend behind the store-house,
The flower-patterned skirt you wanted to try on
And did you ever think
The street in your beloved Hiroshima
Leading to the square would be widened
And named "MacArthur Road"?
And did you think the time would come
When the flapping knotted
Neckerchieves of prostitutes for foreign soldiers
Would flutter through the willows along the
  avenue,
And did you grieve
That even if it had not been for the Bomb,
The war would have ended anyway?

Excerpts from *"An Appeal of All Voices"* Sankichi Toge

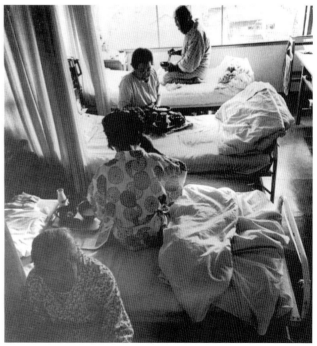

A-bomb survivors repeatedly go in and out of hospitals even now.

A-bomb Disease Still Lingers

Hiroshima
Her face was exposed directly to the A-bomb heat rays and radiation at Zakoba-cho. The scars of her burns led to horrible contracture, so she is unable to shut her mouth by herself.

To a Lady (Excerpts)
Sankichi Toge

Ripped belly uppermost,
A vision of a work-horse kicking the air
Loiters on the stone steps of the water
   trough
At the deserted barracks of the transport corps.

You live hidden, deep in the dilapidated
   alley;
Since that summer, for a year
You only visit the hospital in the train
Hiding beneath an umbrella.

A mass of searing scars
Swooped on your face
From the shadows of B29s
Shining, and now stuck fast
Over your eyes and nose.
You can never face others again,
You say.

In your ruined house you weave
Your life in a skein of blood
With your remaining hand.
What marks of blood will be left
         On your palm?
         A windmill turns gently.
         Children play together
           in the garden
         Of this quiet town.

         Beneath the roar of new
           war-planes,
         I will talk to you
         Of the day when my
           anger
         And your curses
         Will become the most
           beautiful expressions.

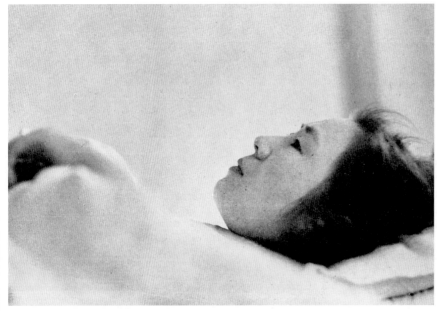

Hiroshima
After the atomic bombing, the loss of hair and diarrhea continued for half a month. She recovered once from these acute effects, but her illness was diagnosed as leukemia six years later.

Japan Became a Center of World Peace Movement

The Movement Against Atomic and Hydrogen Bombs Began in the Peace Struggle of August 6, 1950

Newspaper "Peace Front" Exposed Cruelty of the Atomic Bombs through Photographs for the First Time after the War

Any protest against Atomic bombs was prohibited after the war

This poem of Sankichi Toge (referring to the poem "August 6th") ran in the special issue of the newspaper "Peace Front" published by Akahata (red flag) Chugoku Regional Head Office in Hiroshima. It was for the first time in Japan that the cruelty of atomic bombs was exposed in public through six photographs. Toge's poem was a part of that feature. The newspaper was issued on June 9, 1950. It also reported that an A-bomb photo exhibition was held for the first time in an open space in Hiroshima, writing, "The photo exhibition 'Cruelty of Atomic Bombs' was held in Hatchobori and the place was crowded every day with those people who had lost their relatives."

In another article, it said, "The signature-collecting campaign for peace is widely spreading with the support of trade union youth sections including Hiroshima Shipbuilding Workers' Union, Postal Workers' Union and Hiroshima Streetcar Workers' Union. As of May 28, more than 10,000 signatures are already collected. The Plenary Session of the Hiroshima Prefectural Council of Trade Unions decided on May 28 that the August 6th would be a Day of Anti-War Struggle and called on the affiliated unions and democratic organizations to hold a people's peace rally. Preparations are going on steadily." The article added that preparations were being made also in the neighboring prefectures like Yamaguchi, Okayama, Tottori to organize peace rallies on August 6.

The A-bomb survivors who were struggling for reconstruction of the devastated town were burning with anger at the atomic bomb. They were filled with such deep emotions as they could not describe fully even by using any word or expression. Sometime in 1948, it did not take time for us to understand the fact that when we talked to every unknown person in Hiroshima about the atomic bomb, he or she spoke about how it was almost endlessly without exception, putting aside his or her own business or engagement.

But on the surface there seemed to be nothing. The city was pervaded with the propaganda of mass media that "Hiroshima is working hard for peaceful reconstruction."

"It was inevitable that the atomic bomb should be dropped for the purpose of ending the thoughtless war of the Japanese military and saving the lives of tens of millions of the Japanese people which would have been lost if Japan's mainland should have been reduced to ashes." That was the propaganda which was rampant and suppressed Hiroshima from the sky. The call of "No more Hiroshimas" was forced

The front page of a special issue dated June 9, 1950 of the *"Peace Front."* It carried the poem "August 6th" written by Sankichi Toge.

on us, sounding like "the Japanese should not repeat evil." And it was arranged that this call should be promoted by the U.S.-made Christian churches.

However, all these attempts could not deceive the angry people of Hiroshima who could never forget the question of why their parents, brothers and sisters, husbands and wives, and children should have been massacred by such a horrible weapon. There was no way how to erase the fact that America killed a great number of innocent people in the cruelest way in the history of mankind, making a hell on earth, and how to justify this act. The people of Hiroshima could not see the American soldiers who came to occupy the city irrelevant to the fact that they were a part of the atomic bombers.

(Excerpts from the article *"Hiroshima and Nagasaki"* written by Masayoshi Fukuda and carried by the newspaper "Choshu Shimbun" in 1962)

Atomic Bombing Was Not Necessary for Ending the War

The democratic movement, particularly the peace movement after the end of World War II had to make two tasks clear.

One was to carry out a thorough investigation of the war crimes committed by Japanese imperialism and prevent resolutely our nation from going to war again.

Another was to expose the ambition of U.S. imperialism which occupied Japan after the war.

The war crimes of Japanese imperialism were examined closely and severely by the democratic camp. But the ambition of U.S. imperialism was not fully exposed. It was because basically the democratic camp did not have a clear understanding of the position of U.S. imperialism in the Allied Forces and its stance and policy toward Japan after the war.

The unclear understanding of these matters made the people hesitate about judging whether it would have a historically positive meaning to protest against the U.S. although they were angry at the atomic bombings, that is, massacre of unarmed citizens by the U.S., and, based on their real feelings, they could never tolerate this fact. It was true that there was a one-sided view according to which Japanese imperialism was responsible for the atomic bombings as these resulted from its thoughtless war if the American occupants would promote the democratization of the Japanese society. People's guilty conscience about their "cooperation with the war" acted as a brake on the clarification of the matters.

However, all these interpretations could not deceive the people's masses. How could you erase the undeniable fact that a great number of innocent young and old men and women were massacred! Any explanation was meaningless for the masses.

The Chugoku Regional Committee of the Japanese Communist Party brought to light the crimes of the thoughtless war of aggression committed by Japanese imperialism. At the same time, the regional party committee revealed that U.S. imperialism, hurried by the approaching entry of the Soviet Union in the war, had dropped the atomic bombs to occupy Japan exclusively for its definite program of imperialist aggression and domination, and appealed to the people of the region not to forgive U.S. imperialism under the name of humanity for perpetrating the massacre of innocent unarmed citizens unprecedented in history for that program. The regional party committee also pointed out in its appeal that the Yoshida government had taken the course of militarist revival under the control of U.S. imperialism and turned Japan into a U.S. military base.

(Excerpts from the article *"Hiroshima and Nagasaki"* written by Masayoshi Fukuda and carried by the newspaper "Choshu Shimbun" in 1962)

Voices of the then American leaders

Harry S. Truman
(President of the United States)

"Fini Japs when that (Russia's entry in the Jap war) comes about." (His diary, on the first day of the Potsdam Conference, July 17, 1945)

"(If we use the atomic bomb, I) Believe the Japs will fold up before Russia comes in." (His diary of July 18, 1945 after he received the cable message which confirmed the success of the A-bomb test)

Douglas MacArthur
(Supreme U.S. Commander in the Far East)

"My staff all shared the judgement that Japan was so near to collapse and a surrender might occur at any time." "My military judgement is that the bomb is unnecessary. Japan is preparing to surrender."

Henry L. Stimson
(U.S. Secretary of War, Supreme Commander of the A-bomb operation)

"It was to bring the Japanese surrender at the earliest possible date, before the Russians, who had already entered Manchuria, reached the mainland of Japan."

James F. Byrnes
(U.S. Secretary of State)

"(Mr. Byrnes) did not argue that it was necessary to use the bomb against . Japan in order to win the war .(His) view (was) that (it) would make Russia more manageable..."

But you were unaware
Of what was approaching with
   August 6th.
Starving bands of sick Japanese
   soldiers were
Weaponless in the jungles of the
   South Sea Islands;
Warships short of oil hidden paralyzed
   in the islands;
And the whole nation was bathed
   in a merciless rain of fire
But the fascist commanders of the
   Imperial Army could not end
   the war.

You were unaware
That the eyes of the world saw
Japan's surrender as only a question
   of time,
When the power of Soviets
   smashed the Nazis,
And stopped the ambition of Imperial
   Japan
When the Neutrality Pact expired.

You were unaware
That the swastika's flag-pole lay
   broken
And the red flag raised already
   over Berlin, and
Russia's entry three months later
   into the war against Japan
Fluttered large in the sky of
   history.

"The dropping of the A-bomb was
   precipitated
By the dark ugly motive that
   made them
Smash Japan without Russian aid.
The dropping was precipitated
Because there was only a little
   time left,
After the New Mexico experiment
   on 16 July,
Before Russia entered the war."

This was no accident; no natural
   calamity.
Man's first A-Bomb,
Following a detailed plan and
   rapacious ambition,
Was dropped in a blinding flash
On the Oriental Islands, on the
   Japanese people.
You were killed
Along with 400,000 victims who
   vanished writhing.

Excerpts from *"When Will the Day Come?"*
Sankichi Toge

"Anti-Imperialist and Anti-War Struggle is the Basic Line of the Worker's Movement"

Citizens of Hiroshima held a demonstration to object Korean War in 1950.

The people's mass meeting was held to maintain peace and oppose war at the peace park on the occasion of the first anniversary of the labor dispute of Japan steelworks ten days before the beginning of Korean War, on June 15, 1950. The conference declared main slogan "Oppose the atomic bomb! Don't be useless the death of three hundred thousand People!"

U.S. Imperialism began the Korean War of Aggression June 25th, 1950. The struggle between war and peace result in fierce opponents.

The movement against atomic and hydrogen bombs and the anti-war peace movement headed by the Chugoku district committee of the Communist Party of Japan were started mainly by the working class in the Chugoku district. This movement brought about extensive impacts. Under this movement, for instance, the meeting of young workers in the Chugoku district was held at the Labor Club of Hiroshima Shipyard on July 25th in 1950. There were some forty representatives from twenty one groups, including trade union youth groups and democratic youth organizations from the Chugoku district. After heated discussion, the participants acknowledged the mistakes in their activities up to that point. Then delegates adopted resolutions to adopt anti-imperialism and anti-war struggle as their basic line, and to put this struggle first, beyond only the struggle for improved working conditions and economic benefits, and to strengthen classical propaganda and international solidarity. Finally they resolved to support the Korean National Liberation Struggle and to struggle against the common enemy.

On August 5th in 1950, the day before the August 6th anniversary of the atomic bomb, the young workers decided to hold a Youth Peace Meeting. The slogans of this meeting were as follows:

①Ban the uasage of atomic and hydrogen bombs!
②Any government that initiates nuclear war is a war criminal!
③Achieve national independence by force!
④Do not use atomic bombs against Korea!
⑤Oppose any war that uses young people as human bullets!

At that time the newspaper "The Peace Fighter" reported that the trade union youth group of the Hiroshima Shipyard decided to join the Youth Peace Meeting with half a day strike, and the trade union of Hirosima Electric Railroad took part in the meeting with an all day strike.

(This sentences are quoted from *"Hiroshima and Nagasaki"* written by Masayoshi Fukuda.)

....

Workers, farmers, cultured men and religious people were at the center of the peace movement. The Group of Peace Fighters were formed as the main driving force at factories, offices, schools, regions and agricultural villages throughout the Chugoku district, and the Peace committee were organized around those areas. No movement should base itself on random assertions but rather on well thought out analysis. Forming a movement around famous personages is not a way to construct a healthy strong movement. The movement inevitably spread over a wide area across many different populations. Peace meetings were held throughout the country. However, many meetings were suppressed by policemen. Japanese police oppressed the peace movement of Japanese people on the orders of the U.S. government. Japanese people also had to oppose Japanese ruling classes who supported the Korean War. The active and militant peace-lovimg forces developed resolute struggles to block production and transportation of munitions. A lot of people were arrested during those peace actions.

The development of such peace movements were broadly supported, and the U.S. occupation forces and Japanese reactionary forces couldn't suppress the movements. The August 6th Peace Festival has gathered together a wide range of people year after year since the first August 6th Peace Meeting in 1950, which was besieged by armed policemen. A large number of people assembled at the bomb epicenter on August 6th. Among the people were included those who could not find the bodies of their parents killed by the atomic bomb, those who could not provide their dead with a proper tomb, and those who were forced to keep their anger in their heart silently, without decrying about the outrage. The participants of the peace meeting increased rapidly every year after the first meeting, August 6th 1950.

(This sentences are quotated from "Hiroshima and Nagasaki" written by Masayoshi Fukuda.)

Campaign against A-bomb Began with 1950's Peace Struggle and Developed into a Worldwide Movement

August 6th, 1950
Sankichi Toge

They come running
Running
From everywhere
Pressing the pistols to their sides
Police come running

The center of the city at the Hatchobori junction,
Behind the F Department Store building lay
Waiting expectantly for this day.
But on August 6th, 1950, the Hiroshima Peace Festival was banned;
Shadowy police moving on guard
In the night, at street corners,
At the approaches to the bridges.

Even so
The flow of citizens who had offered flowers
At the memorial monuments and ruins
Soon formed a whirling procession;
Then the sweaty tense faces of police
Plunging into the crowd.
Coerced by the black uniformed line,
The stumbling crowd
Raised their eyes together
To the windows of the fifth and sixth floors
Of the Department Store.
Thousands of leaflets dancing
Here and there
In the air,

Some white, some dark, in the sunlight
Against the summer cloud,
Fluttering down
Everywhere
On their upturned faces
Into their outstretched hands
Sinking slowly into the depths
Of thirsting hearts.

Someone picked one up,
His hand struck, dropped it.
A hand grasped one in the air,
Eyes read it.
Workers, traders, students, girls,
Old men and children of the neighbourhood
Crowd of citizens of the whole city of Hiroshima,
They all share August 6th as a memorial to their dead,
And police,
Push each other and curse
Striving to grasp the peace leaflet
Trying not to be robbed of the Anti-War leaflet
With its sharp appeal!

The trams stop
The traffic lights collapse
Army jeeps roll into the crowd,
The wail of the fire engines' sirens echoes
One after another armed police arrive in trucks.
Through the rows of plain clothes policemen
A foreign army officer's car barges
And the entrance of the Department Store
Becomes a check point for the enemy.

But the leaflets still fall and fall
Slowly and slowly.
When they are caught in the eaves
Hands holding brooms appear
Sweeping them gently down.
One by one, they fall fluttering
As though they were alive,
Voiceless shouts.

At the Peace Festival,
Doves were released, bells rung,
The mayor gave his message of Peace
In the morning breeze.
Now, stamped out like a child's sparkler.
Public lectures,
Concerts,
A UNESCO meeting,
All gatherings banned
And armed and plain clothes police
Occupying Hiroshima.

Smoke from a rocket shell rises
On the cinema screen.
From the back streets reverberates
(Mixed even with children's voices)
The call for an anti-A-Bomb petition.
In the skies of Hiroshima
On August 6th, 1950
Bringing a ray of hope to
The people's dark anxiety
The leaflets flutter
Down and down.
Their shadows fall into the silence of the graveyard
Towards you, who love peace
Towards me, who seek peace.
Drawing the police
They flutter
And flutter.

A peace rally held at Hatchobori, Hiroshima, as a part of the Peace Struggle of August 6, 1950.

The First World Conference Against Atomic and Hydrogen Bombs was organized in Hiroshima in August 1955.

The Movement Against Atomic and Hydrogen Bombs Prevented their Use in their Korean War and the Vietnam War

People held peace march for the twelve mass meeting in Yamaguchi prefecture in July 1966.

The first world meeting against nuclear weapons took place in Hiroshima in August 1955.

The movement against atomic and hydrogen bombs paved a way for itself to combat oppression from the U.S. occupation forces and to expose the crime of the atomic bombings openly in Hiroshima despite suppression under the martial law that existed during the Korean War starting in 1950. This movement spread rapidly all over the country, held a world meeting in 1955, prevented the use of atomic bombs in the Korean War and the Vietnam War, and provided people with the strength not to allow saying that the use of atomic bombs was just.

It is necessary to start a powerful movement against atomic and hydrogen bombs and return to the original 1950 starting point of the anti-atomic bombs struggle. This world-wide movement was a historical accomplishment practically blocking the use of atomic bombs after the war.

That is to say, first, it is most important to respond to the cry of people killed mercilessly by the atomic bombs that is swelling up from the ground, and to join together the fresh outrage of the atomic bomb survivors. No anti-atomic bomb movement can be powerful unless it starts from the anger of the people in Hiroshima and Nagasaki, the only people in the world who only understand the hardship of atomic bombings.

Secondly, it is necessary to dispel the deceptive belief that the atomic bombs were used to end the war, or that Japanese people should not complain against those who dropped atomic bombs and reflect on the acts of aggression. It is equally necessary to completely expose the crimes of those who dropped the atomic bombs.

Thirdly, it is crucial to prevent the U.S., who dropped A-bombs, from trying to use them again rather than apologizing for their acts.

Fourthly, it is necessary to develop strong friendships and relationships of solidarity with peace-loving forces throughout the world, particularly with the people of neighboring countries of Korea and China, which Japan invaded during the war.

Fifthly, it is indispensable to reveal all bogus beliefs and instead offer a correct analysis. These false currents of thought have mistakenly identified an enemy of peace as a friend of peace, and under the pretense of a peace movement have distorted and modified the movement.

And sixthly, workers must take the lead in the peace movement and build a movement involving people from all strata of society such as atomic bomb survivors, youth, women, cultured people, intellectuals, teachers and so on. The labor movement for improved working conditions and economic benefits only is wrong and misguided. The most important duty of the labor movement is the political struggle of all people fighting imperialism and war.

The leaders of China submitted to the U.S. and betrayed the people of the world following the Soviet Union after the 1960's. Under that situation, the movement against atomic and hydrogen bombs was modified and weakened. The leaders of the Soviet Union and China promised "to oppose any atomic weapons" and "to prevent the spread of nuclear weapons", but their common characteristics were not grounded in the angers of the atomic bomb survivors, and not aimed their critique at the United States, who dropped the bombs. The movement against atomic and hydrogen bombs and the movement of the atomic bomb survivors were used as a tool for party interests, self-interest and self-advertisement of some privileged groups, and became their means of making a living. (These sentences are the point of *"Hiroshima and Nagasaki"*)

Movement to Build the "Children's Peace Monument"

Movement to erect the Children's Peace Monument

In October, 1955, Sadako Sasaki, a first-year student in junior high school, died of an A-bomb disease. She was the 12th victim of the A-bomb related children in Hiroshima. Her classmates swore, "No more Sadako! This will never happen again!" Their earnest wish touched young students all around Hiroshima. Soon it turned into a big movement and led to the erection of a child monument, involving the educators of Hiroshima and people nation-wide.

In the month after young Sadako died, her classmates called on the national meeting of the principals of junior high schools to erect a child monument. Furthermore, on the anniversary of Sadako's death her classmates got together to pray for the soul of Sadako and put a kokeshi doll on her grave. Their group is called Kokeshi no Kai, or, in English, A Gathering of Kokeshi Dolls.

In September, 1956, all the boys and girls in Hiroshima City united to organize the Hiroshima Society of Students for Peace. The standing committee was organized by delegates from each school. All students of Hiroshima City were its committee members.

These students stressed to the citizens their intention of erecting a child monument and raised money on the streets.

Some of the members sent proposals for the child monument to many young men in Japan and took charge of the office tasks themselves. Some of the committee members said, "This committee does not belong to any particular members. It belongs to all members." These were their catchwords.

The unveiling ceremony was joined by representatives of students from various places. (1958)

A scene of the party celebrating the unveiling of the Monument.

Rubbed copy "Senbaduru" Inscription on a bell. (Dr. Yukawa Hideki)

Our Declaration

The Children's Peace Monument is a milestone for us in our struggle to build world peace.

Our path to peace does not end here. We hold this monument as a symbol of our prayer for everlasting peace.

Twelve years ago, 12,000 people including our brothers and sisters and some pupils and students of Hiroshima were killed and burnt here. Fourteen of our friends died of illnesses caused by atomic-bomb radiation. How are their souls doing now? Are they pleased to see the memorial monument? Thinking of them, we want to cry out, "No more a-bombs!" "Let no one, anywhere, ever use them again as weapons!"

(Reprinted from the special issue of PEACE No.8 featuring the Dedication of The Children's Peace Monument in May 1, 1958)

A-bomb Survivors' Association of Shimonoseki

A mass movement was launched in February 2001 to present the panels of the "Atomic Bombs and Poems of Sankichi Toge" to the elementary and junior high schools in Shimonoseki city as materials for peace education. A bigger amount of money than expected was donated by people from all strata of society because of their strong support to the movement, so that the panels were presented also to senior high schools in the city and to elementary and junior high schools in a neighboring county.

The Atomic Bomb Survivors' Association of Shimonoseki published in April 2000 a book under the title: "Convey A-bomb experience in Hiroshima and Nagasaki to boys and girls for their peaceful future" and presented 5,400 copies of the book to all the elementary and junior high schools in the city. The book had good educational results.

Students listen to a hibakusha telling her A-bomb experience before their school excursion to Nagasaki.
(At Akada Junior High School, Shimonoseki City in May 2000)

Hibakusha are united for their social mission, not for particular principles and opinions of political groups nor for their own selfish interests. (At the Annual Conference of the Atomic Bomb Survivors' Association of Shimonoseki in May 2000)

With single-minded passion for the sake of the next generation

We, atomic-bomb survivors (hibakusha) of Shimonoseki, have highly appreciated the mission of conveying our experience to young people for peace. We took courage to tell our experience which we had not told even our children. There were also some people who were saying, "We don't have to tell our A-bomb experience. Let us enjoy our remaining years with the allowances we get from the government." But we have chosen the course of working for the public good, for our future generation, no matter how small our contribution may be. We think this is the only way to appease the spirit of the dead.

Last year 49 hibakusha told their experiences to 2,050 people at 22 places in Shimonoseki. Out of them 13 hibakusha spoke in public for the first time. We went to elementary schools, high schools and universities to talk about our experience. We came to be deeply convinced of the significance of our work when we learned later about the impressions of the pupils and students. They listen to us carefully and are touched by our stories. We hear that their attitude has changed a lot both at school and in the home.

When we held the 3rd Shimonoseki A-bomb Exhibition and launched a campaign to present the photo panels to the elementary and junior high schools in Shimonoseki, so many citizens supported our work of conveying to the younger generation the experience that the Japanese should never forget. We owe the success of these events also to the generous and heartfelt support of the newspaper "Choshu Shimbun" which has its origin in the peace movement to ban atomic and hydrogen bombs in 1950 when Sankichi Toge was working, and of the Organizing Committee Against Atomic and Hydrogen Bombs.

We have opposed the tendency to describe the telling of our A-bomb experience as the imposition of our one-sided principles and opinions. We have tried to convey the true voices of Hiroshima and Nagasaki to the younger generation. This is our wish that runs through the photo panels of the Shimonoseki A-bomb exhibition "Atomic bombs and poems of Sankichi Toge" and we are glad to hear that the panels have created a great sensation in Tokyo and Hiroshima.

We feel still now pressure on us when we convey our A-bomb experience. This pressure is put on us through the dissemination of some views which try to seek the reason of the atomic bombing into the fact that Hiroshima was an important military center or justify this act by accusing us that we were assailants as we cooperated the war. But these views are based on the atomic bombers' logic. What do they require us, hibakusha, to reflect on?

We think that those who are in the van of the movement must serve selflessly the whole movement and association. We have abided by the principle that the conflicts between the right and the left wing and the interests of political parties should not be brought in the hibakusha movement. It is because of this principle, I think, that our members have deepened their gratitude and confidence in the executives of the association.

(Speech of Ms. Yukiko Yoshimoto, Chairperson of the Atomic Bomb Survivors' Association of Shimonoseki at a meeting of A-bomb survivors - Aug. 5, 2001 Hiroshima City)

Activities of the Hiroshima Association for the Success of the Atomic Bomb Exhibition "Atomic Bombs and Poems of Sankichi Toge"

The Atomic Bomb Exhibition entitled "Atomic Bombs and Poems of Sankichi Toge" was held from November to December 2001 at the old Bank of Japan, Hiroshima Branch building. To work hand in hand with the Secretariat of the Shimonoseki Atomic Bomb Exhibition toward the success of this exhibit, the Hiroshima Association for the Success of the Atomic Bomb Exhibition "Atomic Bombs and Poems of Sankichi Toge" was formed on October 5, 2001.

The Association has continued to hold this exhibition since 2001 in an attempt to promote a society which will never allow atomic bombs and wars. It is hoped that in telling these stories, the younger generation will come to know the horrors of war, and thus continue our efforts of promoting a peaceful future where wars will be avoided by all means.

The 3 main activities of the Hiroshima Association are the following:

1. Conducting exhibits of the "Atomic Bombs and Poems of Sankichi Toge" panels at various places such as community centers, work places and schools.
2. Communicating, orally and in writing, the experiences of the Atomic Bomb victims to younger generations.
3. Promoting the works of Sankichi Toge.

The number of A-bomb survivors who cooperate in relating their stories has been increasing. They have told their experiences to students who come from other prefectures for school excursions, and to the students in Hiroshima as well.

The old Bank of Japan, Hiroshima Branch building. (2001. November)

Russian students learned the wartime experiences at the Exhibition of A-bomb and War in 2015.

There is growing requests for testimony of the wartime experiences on a school excursion every year. (Pupils of Nishinomiya City Takagi Elementary School in Hyogo prefecture)

Primary schoolchildren hearing the testimony of an A-bomb victim. (Hiroshima city)

"An anthology of the Experiences of Hiroshima A-bomb Victims – After 60 years A-bomb survivors speak out" was published in May 2005. Its English edition also came out and was widely spread.

Caravan Expanded Nationwide!
Evoke the power of peace swirling in Japan

April 18, JR Yokohama Station.   February 13, JR Osaka Station.   May 19, JR Sendai Station.

Many people gathered around the panels. Old people remembered the experiences of the war and the air raids. The youth encountered the truth of the history. (2004~2006)

A-Bomb Exhibition Caravan was formed in February, 2004 and has developed Atomic Bomb Exhibitions on the street, in front of the station and shops, where people gather all over Japan. It is active, year-round, many with the support and cooperation of many people in Shimonoseki City and Yamaguchi Prefecture.

April 18, JR Yokohama Station.

Let's convey the truth of Hiroshima and Nagasaki to the whole country
Street display started in Hiroshima Peace Memorial Park by students of Hiroshima City

The interested students continued the exhibition in Hiroshima Peace Memorial Park since 2011. It shocked people coming from all over Japan and from across the world and created a great sensation.

Many foreigner from all parts of the world visited Hiroshima Peace Park.
The photo below shows foreign young people writing down their impressions of the exhibition in August 2015.

There was a growing tendency toward the opposition movement against Security Act.

The national caravan held street exhibition "A-bomb and War" in Tokyo for three weeks in September 2015. People coming from throughout Japan gathered together the demonstration against the Security Act in front of the Diet, gazed at the exhibition and bought books one after another.

Caravan activity in front of the Diet building.   The street exhibition in front of JR Machida station.   Shopping street in front of Hachiozi JR station.

Nagasaki Association for the Success of the A-Bomb Exhibition

Nagasaki anger breaks the silence

In June 2005, 60 years after the war a panel exhibition on the "Atomic Bomb and Poetry of Toge Sankichi" was held for the first time in Nagasaki. A-Bomb victims began to tell their accumulated angers, breaking the fiction of "Prayer Nagasaki". The atomic bomb exhibition caravan held street exhibitions for 20 days and heard the true voices from the Nagasaki atomic bomb victims.

The second Bomb Exhibition in 2006 was publicized as "Atomic Bomb Exhibition for Nagasaki Citizens." There was much support and cooperation from such organizations as atomic bomb victims, town chairmen, businesses, hospitals, schools and temples. There were also messages from Nagasaki mayor Ito Ichou and Nagasaki governor Kaneko Genjiro, which roused public excitement. Nagasaki bomb victims attended daily, sharing their experiences with each other and with the young people and citizens who volunteered their time to help run the event and work at the reception desk. The event truly was a "bomb exhibition for Nagasaki citizens."

Citizens who experienced the bombing talked together their experiences in front of the Sankichi Toge--A-bomb and War Exhibition.

The slogan "To hear the real voices in Nagasaki" struck a chord with the audience. People began to talk about their thoughts and memories that had been kept inside for 61 years. It was as if a dam had been broken.

Atomic bomb victims and young people also began to act. While the world outside Nagasaki might have previously associated Nagasaki with "prayer," the exhibition provided an avenue for the true thoughts of the citizens of Nagasaki to become a message deeply important to Hiroshima, Japan, and the world.

The hidden strengths of a moving Nagasaki

A campaign to overturn the assassination case of Mayor Ito and to tell the truth Nagasaki, Atomic Bomb and War Exhibit, June, 2007

The Atomic Bomb and War Exhibition in Nagasaki was held under the slogan, "A peaceful future through the continued stories of atomic bomb and war survivors." The event provided a venue for these survivors to share their inner thoughts, demonstrating a continuing resistance to war and to the use of atomic bombs. Their power stemmed from the spirit of Nagasaki citizens who survived the horrors of war and the atomic bomb, re-enlivened by the recent anti-war movement. In the face of potential Constitutional revision, U.S. military realignment, Japanese overseas military missions, increasing legal protection of the public under a wartime regime, and in recognition of the recent assassination of Mayor Ito, the exhibition became a site for activities filled with a spirit, intention, and action that cannot be kept quiet.

At the hypocenter of Matsuyama, Nagasaki city, 10 Nagasaki atomic bomb victims shared their experiences of the bombing to 87 sixth-graders of Shimonoseki Municipal Ichinomiya Elementary School who were visiting on a school trip. The assassination of the Mayor prompted people to share their experiences and thoughts in Nagasaki, which up to this point had commonly been known as "Prayer Nagasaki" for its quieter, more docile attitude.

A-bomb survivors told their experiences to students at the tenth Nagasaki "A-bomb and War Exhibition" in 2015.

A-bomb survivors told their experiences to pupils on a school excursion coming from Kitakyushu City on November 10, 2015.

Everyone Becomes Poor, The Society Looks Like Inviting the Next War

U.S. drove our country Japan into worse conditions

$777 huge fall and chaotic NY stock market. (2008)

From "Sub Prime Shock" to "Leaman Shock", those shocks spread whole globe immediately. In Japan many part time workers lost jobs and a lot of plants had to be closed one after another.

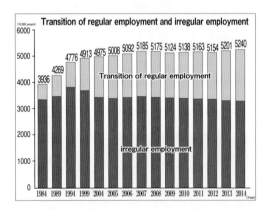

Kinichi Maehara
"Please let me know whether or not about those who delayed paying scholarship loan have some job.
If leaving them, they can't find a good place for working.
We can ask Defense Ministry and give them internship opportunity for a couple of years, so they can find out better jobs.
Defense Ministry says that the office will put it into consider."

(May 2014: at the conference of how to assist for students economically)

Circumstances for children on these days were tough. In an elementary school, 1st grader children cannot eat breakfast, go to school before provided lunch time, going home after eating because parents are working and out of their homes. Parents work part-time jobs, so if they take day-offs, they might be fired anytime. Even in China, the government stopped its one child policy. However in Japan, young parents cannot raise their children in their society now.

Even though terrorism happened in France and Prime Minister Abe said, "I strongly criticize the terror", "Japan is always on the side of France." Listening to the Japanese Prime Minister saying such words, I feel something frightful. Without using money for children and putting them into hard circumstances, the Prime Minister goes to other countries providing huge amounts of money, billions to trillions of Yen, and be directly involved with wars. (Shimonoseki Hibakusha)

Nowadays, there are no places for work in Japan. If you can find some, those working places often provide them with hard labor for a very long time. Many plants are going out of Japan. They are buying food from overseas. In the last war, the conditions were the same. Domestically there were not enough goods, so people are suffering from poverty, then moving to Manchukuo, Indonesia, Philippines, and other Polynesian countries and become popular among the people there. Those who left in Manchukuo had experienced terrible disasters.

Prime Minister Abe and other politicians do not have such war experiences and they are going to the same directions as the last wartime politicians. (female 80's)

Send youth to Self Defense Force

2014
In July, direct mails for asking for joining SDF, sent to all 3rd grade high school students in their home.
The fact appeared that the Defense Force Ministry asked the information about name lists of young people among residents, and 221 (71%) local governments answered to the center government request.
An application form of seeking for SDF members directly arrived at home where junior high school students lived in Okinawa.
2015
Okinawa and Ginowan city governments started to provide the name lists of personal information from 18 to 27 with SDF troop appropriate members.
In Yamaguchi prefecture, 4 high school students who were decided to join SDF, were invited to City Governor's office ,and encouraged. That scene was broadcasted on a cable TV.

An Outline of the Accident of the Fukushima Nuclear Power Plant

On March 11th, the 9.0 magnitude earthquake (intensity 7) occurred off the coast of Sanriku in the Tohoku area. A tsunami of 30 meters hit the Sanriku shore several times.

Tokyo Electronic Company (TEPCO) Fukushima Daiichi nuclear power plant automatically shut down along the earthquake, yet 14 meter tsunami destroyed 12 emergency diesel generator out of 13 and it lost external power supply. Two hours after the earthquake, it lost nuclear reactor coolant system (which is necessary for

avoiding core meltdown) and reactor temperature was raised. Hydrogen explosion occurred in the unit 1, 2, and 3 during March 12th to 15th and the fire broke out on the pool of nuclear spent fuel in the unit 4 (which was under suspension for the periodic check).

Five layered walls trapping the atomic fuel was completely decayed. Meltdown has started 5 hours after the disaster in Unit 1. However the government and TEPCO did not give any information. Radioactivity coming out of Fukushima daiichi plant has already reached to the 1/10 of Chernobyl accident, most of it were released it in early stage of the accident.

People living in with a 20-kilometer radius of the Fukushima daiichi plant and 10-kilometer radius of the Fukushima daini plant were ordered to evacuate after the first explosion on March ("Caution zone"; Futaba town, Ookuma town, Tomioka town, and Naraha town). From May, the government designated additional areas as "Planned evacuation areas" and residents in these areas have been advised to evacuate (Full evacuation of residents; Iidate-6200 people, Katsurao-1600 people, Hirono-5400 people. Partly evacuation; Minamisoma-14200 people, Tamura-380 people, Kawamata-1000 people). 11 communities, total 100,000 people became evacuees. Since there

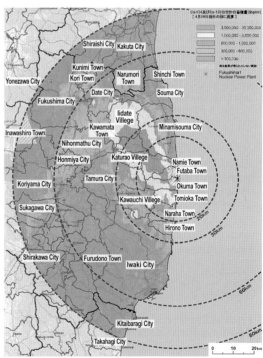

The result of the aircraft monitoring

was no explanation of the influence of the accident, people were taken to the evacuation center with only the barest necessities.

Water accumulating in the basement of the reactor building is contaminated with highly radioactive substances, and the water leaked from the fissured wash port. Moreover, TEPCO dumped 25000 tons of radioactive water into the ocean, which caused damage to the fisheries industry on the Pacific coast including Miyagi, Fukushima and Ibaraki prefectures.

Also, radioactivity have been detected extensively starting with Fukushima, Iwate, Miyagi, Ibaraki, Gunma, Tochigi, Saitama, Chiba, Tokyo, Kanagawa, and Shizuoka. Tap water, feed crop, agriculture product, fishery product, schoolyard, and such are contaminated with radiation of exceeding standard levels. Primary industries are dealt a heavy blow by blocked shipments.

54 Nuclear Power Plants (NPPs) on our Earthquake-prone Archipelago

The early designs of NPPs in Japan were made with no presumption of tsunami and earthquake damage

Shiro Ogura, a former Toshiba nuclear plant design engineer, speaking at the news conference after the disaster said that the first basic thinking behind the Fukushima Dai-1 Nuclear Power Plant design relied on General Electric (GE), which is an American company. Japan later started designing its NPPs presuming the destructive effects of tsunami, but these high waves approximately 10 meters high-- were not anticipated back when he was working on the Fukushima Dai-1 NPP. Ogura also added that it was difficult to speculate how severe earthquakes could affect NPPs.

Introduced GE-made NPPs with no presupposition of tsunami or earthquake

Dale Bridenbaugh, a former General Electric engineer, speaking at an American news show said that the "Mark 1" nuclear reactor design, which was introduced into the Fukushima Dai-1 Nuclear Power Plant from GE, was not designed to withstand such a large-scale accident. Bridenbaugh did not think utilities were taking the fact seriously enough at the time although he felt some of the plants should shut down while the analysis was being completed. GE and the utilities rather did not want to do that, and Bridenbaugh quit his job.

Manhattan Project

A project for the atomic bomb development started on September 17th in 1942 with Lieutenant General Leslie Groves appointed as a supreme commander. The project was named 'Manhattan Project' because the planning headquarters was first to be placed in New York City.

In the same year as the project started, 3 methods to split uranium 235 (centrifuging, gaseous diffusion and electromagnetic separation) were discovered. It was also found that plutonium 239 can be produced from a uranium-graphite reactor and from a uranium-heavy water reactor. With these discoveries, Little Boy, the atomic bomb dropped on Hiroshima, was produced from uranium 235. Fat Man, the one dropped on Nagasaki, was from plutonium 239. The main companies and corporations involved with the production are the following:

E. I. du Pont de Nemours and Company
- designed, built and operated the Hanford Site.

Union Carbide Corporation
- provided enriched uranium utilizing the gaseous diffusion process in the facility that later became the Oak Ridge National Laboratory.

Tennessee Eastman
- provided enriched uranium utilizing electromagnetic separation in the facility that later became the Oak Ridge National Laboratory.

Westinghouse Electric
- manufactured uranium metal.

A critical nuclear accident causes the same radiation injuries as the atomic bomb does

Mr. Shinohara before the accident | Sep.30, 1999 | Oct.10 | Nov.10 | Dec.20 | Jan.4, 2000

Sep. 30, 1999 – His face and arms were exposed to radioctive neutrons because of the accident. The radiation count was 10 sievert per hour (Sv/h).

Oct. 10 – Some symptoms like red spots, vomiting, diarrhea and disorder of consciousness appeared although there was no external wound.

Nov. 10 – 70% of his skin peeled off.

Dec. 20 – Some grafts of skin were implanted to his forearms.

Jan. 4, 2000 – Some more grafts of skin were implanted also to his face, but his skin could not regenerate.

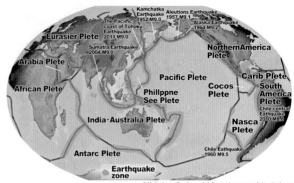

All "plate" should be changed to "plate"

Henry Stimson, Secretary of the Army

"We did not regard it merely as a new weapon but as a revolutionary change in the relations of man to the universe and that we wanted to take advantage of this; that the project might even mean the doom of civilization or it might mean the perfection of civilization; that it might be a Frankenstein which would eat us up or it might be a project 'by which the peace of the world would be helped in becoming secure'.(May in 1945)

Peaceful Use of Nuclear Energy Campaign promoted by U.S.

After the war, America started developing a power reactor and a nuclear ship reactor while trying the development or experiment of a new hydrogen bomb. After Manhattan Project, the American Atomic Energy Commission exclusively managed research and development of a nuclear power reactor.

The development of a power reactor was sold off to a non-governmental group in 1953, and private electrical manufacturers built a nuclear power plant, and that is how electric companies started owning their own NPP and operating it.

Nuclear plant manufacturers such as Westinghouse Electric (WH) and General Electric (GE) appeared. After the war, though GE was in the project for the development of the nuclear ship reactor, the company chose a boiling water reactor as a power reactor, and the "Mark 1" was introduced to Fukushima Dai-1 Nuclear Power Plant.

Both of GE and WH started business activity in the department for NPPs and marketed in Japan while they contracted American government projects in the department for nuclear weapons. Matsutaro Shoriki followed them in Japan, and Yasuhiro Nakasone went after him.

Tetsuo Arima, a professor of Waseda University

Media campaigns such as 'mission for the peaceful use of atomic energy' of Yomiuri Shimbun and Nippon Television in the earlier 1955 and 'nuclear disarmament exhibition' in the later 1955 were instigated by Matsutaro Shoriki and the American secret services. The purposes of America were; 1) achieve the 'atoms for peace' policy of President Eisenhower in Japan, 2) tone down the anti-atomic-hydrogen-bomb campaign and anti-America sentiments, 3) convince the Japanese Prime Minister to have nuclear weapons in the country. To achieve these purposes, America had to change the Japanese strong 'nuclear allergy' brought about by the atomic bombs dropped on Hiroshima and Nagasaki, and the Dai-5 Fukuryumaru accident.

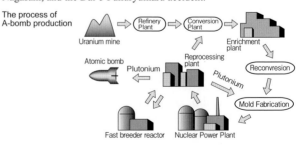

124

Shut Down All the Nuclear Power plants in Japan

Japan has now entered a period of brisk seismic activity

▶ The government and some media told us "The radioactivity won't impact on your health immediately, there's no need to worry". Famous scholars from Hiroshima and Nagasaki even said, "Don't worry, it's less harmful than cigarette." But one day, the government ordered us to move out from the village. I believe this crisis situation is caused by the nation and Tokyo Electric Power Company, if we must move out they should take full responsibility for it. My whole body shook with anger. (Iidate village/Farmer, male)

▶ It was snowing in Iidate village on that explosion day, and which increased the radiation dose. At that time amount of radiation was much higher than today, but we were ignored for long time, and now they said we must leave the village. What is it all about? Cattle are just like a family for us, we can't kill them easily.
(Iidate village/ Cattle farmer)

▶ Tokyo Electronic Power Company told us Iidate village is located on strong foundation rock and therefore it is an "earthquake-proof village". They have suggested the plan to make an underground nuclear-waste repository in our village for couple of years. (Iidate village/Farmer, male)

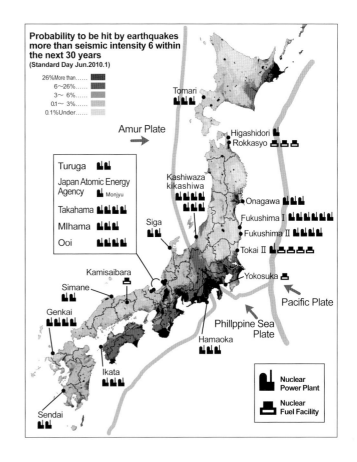

A statement of Katsuhiko Ishibashi
(Seismologist / Professor of Kobe University at the time)
at the hearing of the Diet

There is a pattern of earthquake in Japan, "seismic activity" and "seismic quiescence". There is a geographical and physical basis for it. Now, I have to mention the historic fact, which is Japan experienced a postwar remarkable reconstruction, high economic growth, and developing technologies (that brought a city greater convenience and population concentration) in seismic quiescence by chance. In other words, modern Japanese nation and society were created without suffering a massive earthquake and therefore we could say we have fragile state foundations toward to earthquake. Now, most of the seismologists share common perceptions that Japanese archipelago enter a period of brisk seismic activity of large earthquakes. We are now facing a risk of being struck by strong earthquakes for the first time in our history. And it is not just one but there will be a number of times.

"Condo without a toilet"

The Fukushima I nuclear disaster showed that used and being tested fuel rods were stored in pools of water at the top of the each reactor building.

54 nuclear power plants have been built in Japan without enough provisions against final disposal of radioactive waste. It's obvious that radioactive materials come out the plants if it started, therefore many experts have warned of the recklessness using the term "Condo without a toilet".

Rokkasho village reprocessing plant, costing some JPY 2 trillion, is still not fully operational and most of the spent fuel are reprocessing under contract in France. After extracted plutonium and uranium, there remains worthless high-level waste. There is no specific final disposal site for this high-level waste and those are kept accumulating.

Katsuhiko Ishibashi
(Professor emeritus at Kobe University)

Ever-increasing spent reactor fuel is high-yield and it must be insulated from living environment. It is called "Nuclear trash". After the reprocessed, it is necessary to store the package on the surface for 30 to 50 years to allow a sufficient temperature and radioactivity decrease before disposing of them underground (over 300meters deep). And then all we could do is to wish the rock trap radioactivity for over a hundred thousand years. I believe this formation disposal is a bet on a lame rooster that surely causes enormous amount of trouble for the future generation. There is no telling where earthquakes will be in coming hundred thousand years, regardless of active faults near the earth's surface.

Fukushima Can Certainly Revive

Reconstruction work of city train in the vicinity of Kamiya-cho crossing about 400 m away from the hypocenter of explosion. (Hiroshima-city, October 1945)

By the end of August after the bombing, the black-market had already formed and was full of people. (Hiroshima-city, Spring 1946)

▼We A-bomb survivors lived in Hiroshima without knowing even the presence of radioactivity, drinking radioactively-contaminated water, and surviving by eating tomatoes grown there. A lot of people were lost to diseases such as leukemia. In the midst of all of this, though, we had no choice but to rebuild our own hometown by ourselves. Although it was said that Hiroshima would remain a barren field for at least 70 years following the bombing, plants now sprout from the ground.
Currently, people know what radioactivity is, and are confronted with the figure of 'Sieverts'. They in turn fear what we knew nothing about. This fear is compounded by the fact that the government does not provide their citizens with accurate information to make informed decisions. There have been stories in the news of children being discriminated in Tokyo and sent back to their hometowns, all because they are from Fukushima. This discrimination too is the responsibility of the nation which has never taken seriously the dangers of radioactivity. We survivors of Hiroshima continue to suffer discrimination even now, 65 years since the bombing.
(Hiroshima-city, 80s, man-bomb victim)
▼Following the bombing, Nagasaki's situation was sufficiently dire that it was labeled an atomic field. We were able to rebuild Nagasaki to what it is today because we grew potatoes and squash in those burned fields and because we were blessed with an abundance of seafood. Even with electricity or money, human beings die if they lack food. The nation has emphasized our need to import food. I think instead we should benefit from our experience of Japan's postwar construction and learn to support ourselves.
(Nagasaki, 80s, Female-bomb victim)
▼Cannot bear the thought of people who were suddenly expelled from their homes. The national government intends to permanently expropriate the land in contaminated areas, but people have reconstructed Nagasaki, including the hypocenter of the bombing. I recently found a film which was taken 10 years after the bombing. What I can see in that film was that a lot of huts are lined up although buildings were not constructed and the town was full of people. Even 2 months after the bombing, Nagasaki Kunchi was as full as it had been in the past. The town was full of people eager to preserve local history and cultures even through difficult times. In case of Fukushima, air and soil were contaminated, but the town was not burned down. If Tokyo Electric Power Co., Inc. or the national government compensates citizens and they have the will to turn people's lives back to normal as an instrument of national policy, I am certain people can return to their homes.
(Nagasaki-city, 70s, Female-bomb victim)

▼My mother died from burns suffered over her entire body. I also continuously had hair loss and my gums bled and suffered from thyroid disease. We were left in the ashes of the atomic bomb, but we have been continued to survive, going so far as to drinking mud and eating weeds, all the while appreciating the ability of humans to live through horrible circumstances and thinking of my mother, brother, and sisters, all of whom died in my stead in the bombing. All of Japan showed a similar fortitude following the war, starting from nothing, saying to themselves, 'We will work to prevent our children or grandchildren from experiencing what we experienced.' However, Japan has followed U.S. dictates. We have renounced our war responsibility. In war time, Japan forced its citizens to say 'We have no wants until we win' and taught us to sacrifice ourselves for the nation. Nevertheless, Japan has simply followed the U.S., eating away at the nation itself. The U.S. has not treated Japan as equals; the bomb victims were treated like laboratory rats. Unless the current politics of Japan are changed, people in Japan will face a future crueler than the hell of the atomic bombs.
(Nagasaki-city, 80s, Female-bomb victim)

Voices of A-bomb Victims

▼The victims of Fukushima and the A-bomb have both been treated like things, not people. The victims of the A-bombs could not express their anger and pain because of the discrimination they felt. The nuclear power plants in Japan were made because of American pressure.
(Nagasaki-city, female A-bomb victim in her 80s)

▼There was temporary sympathy, but at the time Nagasaki had no choice but to use their own power to survive. It is the role of the country to support its people. We should make our government take responsibility for the future of Japan.
(Nagasaki-city, 81 years old, woman)

▼We built housing while being told, "trees and plants will not grow in Nagasaki." I, however, have grown my potatoes here for 70 years. The people of Fukushima can evacuate the area and change the soil, but this is only temporary. The problem is if Japan has the will to help Fukushima.
(Nagasaki-city, male A-bomb victim)

▼The day after the A-bomb fell, my father collected wood and began to rebuild our home. We rebuilt Hiroshima after the bomb because it was our home. I think the people of Fukushima feel the same way. The government told use to evacuate, and gave us temporary housing, told us what to do and where to go. But we did not want to be ordered around. We must eat fish and even though there is radioactivity in the sea, we will live there and eat the fish.
(Hiroshima-city, Hibaku-Nisei, woman)

Distribution of food in the neighborhood of Matsuyamamachi, Nagasaki-city railroad crossing

[Timeline of the Hiroshima-city revival]

1945
August 6,	the atomic bomb was dropped
August 24,	the opinion that for 70 years nothing will grow
September,	Makurazaki typhoon came and flooded Hiroshima. 80% of bridges were washed away and shelters were destroyed.
October,	Streetcar service was restored and construction of temporary housing began.
November,	The Ebisu Shrine was rebuilt and the festival was held. Each neighborhood office was rebuilt, and a market began in front of Hiroshima station. Citizens had built over 5000 new houses within 6 months.

1946
January,	City hall was reconstructed.
April,	Gas was restored.
May,	Water was restored to 70% of service. Food was scarce, so people made dumpling with grass and seaweed to eat. Small gardens were popular and many people grew pumpkins and potatoes.

1947
January,	The population reached 200,000 people.

[Timeline of the Nagasaki-city revival]

1945
August 9,	the atomic bomb was dropped.
August 12,	the train between Michinoo and Nagasaki was reopened.
August 14,	Electricity was restored.
August 26,	Urakami Station reopens, and business resumes.
September,	The government states the land will be unusable for 70 years. They told citizens to evacuate, but people did not go.
	Ally forces arrived in Nagasaki and opened the Kyushu Shipping Bureau office in Nagasaki office.
October,	Nagasaki Kunchi Festival is held in Suwa Shrine .
	Nagasaki bus service reopens.

1946
Nagasaki fish market starts.

1947
January,	Complete restoration of Nagasaki bus service.
December,	Sardine Cannery is reopened.

1950
The population of Nagasaki exceeds 240,000 people.

Incidents Involving Japanese People Taken as Hostages in the Middle East

Japanese government policy contributed to hostage taking

Prime Minister Abe (Japan)

"It is regrettable that such a terrible incident had happened. We should condemn the terrorists. The terrorists have to take responsibility. Therefore, Japan continues to cooperate with other countries and institutions. We will never yield to terrorism. The Japanese government will prepare laws to allow the Japan Self-Defense Forces to rescue Japanese people when they receive serious threat."

Prime Minister Abe announcing a $200,000,000 aid in front of the national flag of Israel 1/17/2015

President Obama (U.S.)

"We should prevent another land war in the Middle East. We will weaken this terrorist organization, and finally, exterminate it through a coalition of nations."

88 year-old man who is a survivor of the atomic bomb
(Hiroshima)

"Prime Minister Abe visited Israel which is surrounded by many hostile countries and declared $200,000,000 donations to Israel. This was followed by a hostage taking event so think this incident was caused by the Japanese government's policy. Moreover, a second Japanese person was taken as a hostage last November.

Japan was exposed to radiation and the Japanese people had experienced a lot of difficulties during the wartime. It was America that dragged Japan into the war. It is obvious that from now on Japanese people and companies in foreign countries can encounter dangerous conditions more easily. To make matters worse, the Prime Minister wanted to invoke a self-defense policy but this endangers the people even more.

Prime Minister Abe donated $200,000,000 easily just like it is from his own pocket money. In reality that money came from tax paid by the citizens. In the end, they could not find any ways to save those hostages. The Japanese government always invokes the slogan "human life is first" so I insist that rescuers must not come back to Japan until they can save those hostages."

Man who was a sailor (Shimonoseki-shi)

"I worked on trawl boats in Senegal in West Africa and Mozambique in southern Africa from the 1960's.

I usually worked with Africans and there was no one who spoke ill of Japanese people at that time. When I brought a ship alongside a quay and was doing an unloading operation, a lot of Africans were gathering around me. I still remember that they repeatedly said "please stay here" when I was about to leave Senegal. I assume that Japanese people were respected there because of some reasons. One is that Japanese people are earnest, hard workers and don't usually lie. The other is that Japan reconstructed their country after losing the WWII

Japan should contribute to world peace in ways different from America. If Japan Self - Defence Forces work with the U.S. Army, the relationship based on trust between us and African countries would be lost completely."

Osamu Miyata
(the managing director of Center for Contemporary Islamic Studies, teacher of the University of Shizuoka)

"Today, the media always report barbarism committed by the IS. However, the Iraq War was the largest and harshest event for the Iraqi people. This war was caused with no justified reasons and 190,000 people (their families, relatives and members of their same tribes) were killed by the U.S. Army (the number of victims killed in this war is estimated by others to be between 500,000 to 600,000).

Most people don't know the truth of the Iraq War because of media blackout. For instance, a daisy cutter which was used by the U.S. Army during the Iraq War can burn up a much wider area than a napalm bomb. Its destructive power is very strong.

The Iraq Army compared it to an atomic bomb. Of course, the incident wherein a Jordanian pilot was burned alive is cruel but how about thousands of people who were also burned to death by the daisy cutter. It was tragedy, wasn't it?

From the point of view of the Iraqi people, Japan had never sent its military unlike European countries. In addition, once they meet Japanese people, everybody say "Two atomic bombs were dropped on Hiroshima and Nagasaki by America." It is usual for Japanese media not to mention who dropped the atomic bombs. On the other hand, Arab people don't evade the subject. They are surprised with Japan that experienced a rapid economic development and progress of modern technology after the WWII.

The Koizumi government supported the Iraq War and sent the Self - Defence Forces of Japan there at the first instance. I think that the Koizumi government and the Abe government spoiled the relationship based on trust between Japan and the Middle East."

Eiji Nagasawa
(professor of Institute for Advanced Studies on Asia, the University of Tokyo)

"The primary factor is the attack on Iraq and failure of dealing with the Iraq War by the American and the British Army. In recent times, the major issue in the Middle East is that western countries intervened militarily again and again. In addition, the failure of building modern nations has promoted the ideology which established more Islamic order.

I do not think that democratization like Western countries is the only proper way. It depends upon Arabs to choose the best way of governance

Japan is an independent state so the Japanese government should continue with omnidirectional and peaceful diplomacy. Recently, Japan ruined the lessons of WWII. Arabs have favorable impressions on Japan. We have to emphasize that Japan is a peace-loving nation a lthough we have the U.S. bases. But we will not use its military and are always keenly conscious about the atomic bomb incident ever since. I wish that Japanese and Islamic people will have an opportunity to know each other better through this incident concerning hostages.

Abe Government Proceed to The Security Legislation

The speech of the Prime Minister Abe at the U.S. Congress, April 30, 2015

"Now, Japan is trying to enrich the Security legislation. After its realization, Japan will be able to cope with measurable emergencies continuously. Through this, the cooperative relationship between the Japan Self Defense Forces and the U.S. Army will be strengthened and Japan-U.S. Alliance will be stronger. It will provide a certain deterrence that will result to peace of the regions.

It is the first big reform after the WWII. We have decided that we are going to fulfill our responsibility more and more for the peace and stability of the

April 30.2015

Japan Self Defense Forces

world, so definitely, we have determined to promulgate the bill by this summer. "The Positive Pacifism based on the Principle of International Cooperation" will be the guideline for our actions in the future."

The Press Conference of Prime Minister Abe, May 14

"Only a country cannot protect the safety of the country any longer. In the situation in which the U.S. Army is attacked around Japanese waters, there is some possibility that Japan also is exposed to risks. These are just our own risks."

"There is no possibility that Japan is involved in the wars waged by the U.S. Army. We use the armed forces only for protecting the Japanese people. It is wrong to call the Security legislation as the "War Bill" without bases. It will never happen from now on that the Japan Self Defense Forces join the Gulf War and the Iraq War."

The Secretary of State, John Kerry
(receiving the revision agreement of the Guidelines for Japan-U.S. Defense Cooperation)

"Not only defending their own areas, Japan has established the capacity to defend U.S. and another partners, if necessary. It is a historical turning point of Japan-U.S. defense relationship."

The Secretary of Defense of the United States, Ashton Carter

"The new guideline does not have geographic restrictions. It has become global from formerly pointed confined areas."

The Minister of Defense, Nakatani
(June 5, The House of Representatives Peace and Security Legislation Special Committee)

"We have decided based on the discussion at a cabinet meeting how we apply the Constitution of Japan to the bill."

The Vice-President, Takamura
(May 5, at a program in NHK)

There is no kerosene in Japan and many people froze to death in cold districts. This is a situation in which "the right of the people is radically overridden".

July 15, The Steamrolling of the House of Representatives
(The Prime Minister, Abe July 15, at the interpellation in the morning)

"Unfortunately, the people have not understood yet."

The Special Advisor to The Prime Minister, Yosuke Isozaki
(July 26, at the national administration debriefing in Oita city)

"There is no relationship between the constitutional interpretation and legal stability. We have to mind whether it needs the steps for protecting our country or not. It is the constitutional interpretation of the government, so if necessary, it should change with the transitions of the times."

Explanation of the right of collective self-defense and the legal institutions about security in Japan by Prime Minister Abe

"Figuratively speaking, the legal institutions about security should fasten the doors securely. In former times, closing the shutters is enough to defend against the thief and protect our property. However, new ways of stealing are occurring today. For example, phone scams or identify theft result to the electronic stealing of some people's estates. We must always prepare for such a situation. If we lock the doors to provide against emergencies, evil people would give up the idea of invading Japan."

"When my friend Mr. Suga calls and demands from me to save him from the robber, I can't go to his house and help him. The reason is that it is not considered as the crisis of (Japanese) existence. On the other hand, there are some delinquents who try to hit Mr. Abe because he is impertinent. One day, Mr. Abe is walking with his friend Mr. Aso and then a bad person struck Mr. Aso. In that case, he can rescue Mr. Aso. This is an example of the right of collective self-defense."

The Campaign to Prevent Another
Never let the young Japanese people

Appeal by the Association of Scholars Opposed to Security-related Bills

In violation of Article 9 of the Constitution, these bills would provide for Japan's Self-Defense Forces to cooperate actively with U.S. and other foreign military operations overseas. We very strongly appeal for the Diet to consider them most carefully and to reject them in keeping with the Constitution.

We carry a special historical burden in that universities collaborated with Japan's war of aggression and sent numerous students off to battle. Profoundly repentant of this history, we have adopted Article 9 as our own, have engaged in research and education as the bedrock for world peace, and have worked so as to never again be visited by the horrors of war. We cannot allow a situation to arise anew in which our young people are sent off to war to kill and be killed. In the name of scholarship and conscience, we most strongly protest these unconstitutional legislations submitted to the Diet and are appalled that they are even being deliberated by the Diet. We stand in resolute opposition to this legislation.

Appeal by Volunteers from Kyoto University

War starts in the name of defense
War makes a lot of money for the armament industry
War soon goes out of control
War is easy to start but hard to stop
War brings harm to children and seniors as well as soldiers.
War leaves a deep scar on our lives mentally as well as physically
Human psyche is not an object to manipulate
Human life is not a hapless pawn.

Sea must not be destroyed by military bases

Urgent symposium in Kyoto University (July 14, 2015)

Masukawa Toshihide (Kyoto University, physics, Nobel laureate)

A lot of Japanese people have come to stand out in opposition to the laws in a short time, which reminded me of the Japanese national campaign against the Security Treaty in 1960. Considering the historical context, after Japan's defeat in World War II, the U.S. occupation army came here, and then the basic policy of America was to make Japan a second-class nation which cannot wage war any more. However, a revolution occurred in China soon after and the Korean War broke out. In the meantime the United States encouraged Japan to be militarized again and Japan was regarded as a bulwark against communism. Despite all those happenings, Article 9 of the Constitution has remain unchanged.

It should be noted that the trend being reversed, the Abe Cabinet's approval rating is quickly declining. People become aware of how dangerous Prime Minister Shinzo Abe's underhanded scheme is. We can make war once he judges it as a military emergency, although it should be done after the Constitution is revised by replacing Article 9 with another one. His view is really antagonistic to constitutionalism. I see, however, bright prospects for the future. Rising chorus of opposition in just the past week we heard, so we should expand it throughout the county and give the Cabinet a hard blow. I believe we should keep on fighting until Shinzo Abe resigns. The Liberal Democratic Party has had various statespersons including ultra-rightists, but I have never seen such an irresponsible and slapdash politician as Shinzo Abe. He must resign right now.

Ikeuch Satoru (Nagoya University, Cosmophysics)

The Security-related Bills suggest an aspect of the Abe Cabinet's remilitarization policy. The Cabinet has also been making a serious impact on our lives in various fields. For example, scientists and researchers will be encouraged to cooperate with military research. The Science Council of Japan declared in 1950 and 1967 that we would not carry out any study for war or do military researches, based on the lessons we learned from World War II, when the researchers assisted the war effort. Universities and research institutions in Japan have seldom done military researches ever since. We embody the spirit of the Constitution by not carrying out any research for military purposes. However the Abe Cabinet encourages us to carry out military research. The national universities have been impoverished owing to the budget being curtailed. The researchers have been short of money for their study, which leads them to military research. We have social responsibility, that is, a duty to act for the benefit of society. We thus declared that our researches must be used for making people happy and achieving peace. Any military research might turn into a secret research. That is why we decided never to get involved in military researches. We want to expand such a movement.

War is Spreading Nationwide
become human bullets for the U.S.

Sky must not be destroyed by the roaring noise of a jet-fighter

We would like to live a life in an unusual country where knowledge production is boasted rather than in a normal country where the shedding of blood as an international contribution is boasted.
Learning is not a weapon of war
Learning is not a tool of business
Learning is not a servant of power

We must strike a heavy blow to the persons in power who are being unduly vain and conceited so that we can protect and create our place to live and think freely.

It was filled with many people especially the youth in front of the Diet. (July. 2015)

▶Those who have no understanding of what constitutionalism is govern politics. It is nothing but fascism that the legislative body ignores the Constitution by changing a prime minister's personal wish into the necessity of the nation. It is obvious that they govern along the lines of U.S. However the prime minister is now intimidated. I appreciate the students who are beginning to do a campaign against the laws. Building the national opinion by supporting those students will lead to our victory. I will fight with them.
(Man of 30's, Tokyo)

▶I joined this because I found a sign board announcing the campaign. I am filled with a sense of danger. Although I have been indifferent to the society, I found that if I do nothing concerning the laws, I would be involved in the situation of killing or being killed. Peace Research Institute is on our campus, where the teachers taught us that the noble purposes of World WarⅡ were "the protection of Japanese people abroad" and "securing of resources", which are just the same as Abe Cabinet is insisting concerning the security-related bills. Who else are opposed to the bills but students? Some say opposing the laws is bad for us in getting a job. I joined this meeting, determined to turn down such a company as not to choose those students.
(A 19-year-old student)

▶I watched TV and knew that the bill had been rail-roaded. So I have rushed over here. The government ignored the will of the people in 1960, which I learned in a history class. The same thing is happening now. As a high school student, I think it is wrong to remain silent. I don't want this movement to end in vain. I would respect the result if the Constitution was changed in a referendum. However, why should we follow Mr. Abe's private opinion? (A high school student)

War veterans and A-bomb victims
▶Prime Minister Shinzo Abe's speech to Congress of the U.S. was far from appropriate because he promised to pass the Security-related bills which enable us to exercise the right of collective self-defense. We have not discussed it in the Diet yet and Mr. Abe has not appealed to the county concerning the issue. He advertised himself in the speech, saying how hard he worked for the U.S. He is just a ridiculous man.

"Enactment of an independent Constitution", "positive pacifism" or "for protecting people's lives" are Prime Minister Abe's empty platitudes which will shut our mouth up. Moreover he is willing to respond to the demands from the U.S. He is doing this by endangering our lives, which is just opposite to our wish. His idea that he is a sovereign is alien to our idea of a democratic country. Which government does he belong to? (A-bomb victim, Hiroshima)
▶The right of collective defense or enactment of an independent Constitution Shinzo Abe has advocated will lead us to war although he believes he can defend our country and secure peace with it. He insists on military expansion because the tension between Japan and China has been increasing. But I believe that the Japanese people experienced the miseries of the war and so we should establish a friendly relationship with Chinese people who also experienced the same horrible war-time lives as victims. Nagasaki has thus achieved progress in social development. Prime Minister Shinzo Abe will never take responsibility just as the rulers shifted all the responsibilities for the Second World War to all the Japanese by using the phrase "a national confession of Japanese war guilt".
(Man, Nagasaki)

Calling for the breakaway

Surge of the public opinion against nuclear power plant

The nuclear politics which arose from the atomic bombing

While Japan is now full of nuclear power plants, I have come to know for the first time the course followed by the nuclear energy policy introduced after the war.

America dropped atomic bombs so as to occupy Japan and she is seemingly an independent country whose situation has virtually become like an American colony. The government is going to restart nuclear power plants even though the recovery from the aftermath of the explosion accident of the Fukushima Nuclear Power Plant has not been made yet. The city planning for "recovery and reconstruction after the disaster" is only meant for a small group of people holding business interests with the local people ignored and all left angry. The second "tsunami" of consumer tax increase and so forth that threatens citizens' life has also struck them. I would like the next generation of youngsters to be concerned about changing the evil trend of the present society. (Sendai city, man in his 70s)

We cannot keep providing bases for U.S. military endlessly

American bombers flew over Korea after air raiding Japan. Many of my seniors at school were killed in the war as kamikaze squads and I was also going to join one. In the Great Iwakuni Air Raid carried out on the day before the end of the war, many of my friends lost their mothers or had all their families and relatives exterminated. America, knowing the imminent conclusion of the war, carpet bombed Iwakuni citizens as though trying to use up their excess bombs and burned the people to death. Do they regard the citizens of Iwakuni or the Japanese as worms or anything? It is impossible to let Japan provide bases for the U.S. military indefinitely. Learning a lesson from the horror and misery of the past war and never to have it repeated, America and her follower, the traitorous Japanese government have to be purged. (Iwakuni city, man in his 60s)

Japan won't change by turning the Japanese government into an American subordinate

The present government is the same as the one in the Second World War, which cheated the people of Japan through fake news called "Imperial Headquarters radio news release." In the case of the explosion accident at Fukushima nuclear energy plant, the government has only kept protecting "Toden," and made the living condition of the victims even more difficult by raising electricity charges. There are nuclear power plants all over Japan, but these were forcibly sold to Japan by America after the war and this seems to mean to have confined and subjugated all the Japanese with nowhere to escape. The TPP is also a policy only for a few major companies to increase their profit, totally disregarding the people in the farms and fishing industries and smaller businesses. It is ridiculous that the government tries to implement policies where no considerations are given for the current situation of the Japanese citizens. There is no way for Japan to change by turning to the Japanese government, an American subordinate, no matter who becomes the prime minister. The world has become a place where hard working people are treated like material things, even though the society cannot go on without them. If politics are run from the viewpoint of many working people, Japan will become a much richer country. The youngsters should stand up for that.

(Tokyo, male in his 20s)

The beach of Oshika Town in Ishinomaki City that continued in a vacant lot.

Don't let the sky of our homeland become a war zone.

Initially there appears to be a base of the Self Defense Party, but America is hiding behind it. Once an American base is established, then the situation will be obvious by looking at Okinawa. The Abe regime accepts and swallows whole American demands like a pet cat swallowing a fish and is even trying to change the constitutional interpretation as in the past. How can it be "for the peace of Japan?" What Okinawa doesn't need, Saga doesn't need either. A resident's association is an organization to help activate local communities and insuring a secure and safe life. A plan that threatens to undermine its basic concepts cannot be accepted.

(Saga city, Kawamitsu cho, President of resident's association)

There is an increasing tendency toward demonstration against TPP all over Japan.(Iwate Prefecture)

from colonial rule of the U.S.

reoperation, consumption tax increase and TPP

Excerpts from "About the Two Ruins"
Ritsumeikan University Professor Emeritus Nagao Nishikawa

"We now know as historical facts about how the American military hid the information of the damage of A-bombings and nuclear tests and how America, the Japanese government and business sector have publicized the safety and efficiency of the peaceful use of atomic energy with the help of nuclear experts and news media. In addition, we know how huge amount of money has been thrown around in order to suppress the anti-war, anti-nuclear and anti-violence movements brought about by the horrible memories of the war, Hiroshima and Nagasaki and furthermore the A-bombed Fifth Fukuryu Maru. Peaceful use is a disguised war-time technology and a horrifying scheme of big money capitalists."

"The Great East Japan Earthquake has revealed the colonialism structure in Japan and the world all at once......Present relationship between America and Japan is plainly shown in the system of peaceful use (nuclear energy plant) under a nuclear umbrella."

"Post war period seems to have come to a disastrous end at last. The complete process cycle of 'long post war period' must be strictly reviewed."

American food strategy

Former President Bush's speech to farmers

"Food self-sufficiency ratio is directly related to national security. America is so lucky to sustain it appropriately all the time because of you. Could you imagine any country which cannot self-support food? I imagine you know which country I am talking about. Countries unable to self-support food are vulnerable to international pressure and risks."

A lot of People held the rally for the election for governor in Okinawa Prefecture on November 1, 2014. The site was filled with enthusiasm for removal of the U.S. military base.

Cooperation work of the fishermen of Iwate prefecture.

A speech quoted from a classroom lecture
Wisconsin State University Professor of Agricultural Economics

"American agricultural products are political weapons. So produce inexpensive, high quality products and they can become tools to control the world."

"Certain small country on the east sea has very diligent people. However, it's inconvenient for us if we let them work freely. So, lure them by food to their destination."

Corruption in Colonialism
2007 Report from "General research project of preventive measure for lifestyle diseases including cardiovascular disease," sponsored by the Ministry of Health, Labor and Welfare

"The prevalence rate of pathological gambling of our country is 9.6%."
(The prevalence rate of pathological gambling for developed countries is 1.5~2.5%)

There are more English class hours than Japanese language class hours in the junior high school curriculum.

There are 385 class hours in three years for the Japanese language and 420 class hours in three years for English. Comparing with the former status, Japanese language class hours increased from 350 to 385, English from 315 to 420, representing a major increase. In elementary schools, one hour a week English education for fifth and six graders has been introduced for real.

Civil Protection Law Allows Nuclear Arms Use

The Civil Protection Law was enacted in 2004 as a part of "Emergency Related Seven Laws". It imposes upon each prefecture and municipality a duty to make "Civil Protection Plan" based on a national guideline to establish measures that shall be taken in preparation against armed attack or in response to ongoing attack. Among the cases of "armed attack situations", not limited to only guerrilla warfare and the offensive by special-forces but also the attack by ballistic missiles and nuclear weapons are specified.

Disaster Prevention Drills based on the national protection plan.
(May, 2008, Yukuhashi-city, Fukuoka Prefecture)

"Lee to avoid and escape in a raincoat"
-----quoted from the national guideline

"Escape to a secured basement when you sense the attack", "When a sharp flash shines, cover both ears and hide behind buildings". "When fleeing, avoid ground zero and the lee and while reducing external exposure to radioactive fallout with gloves, hats and raincoats, etc., you should also strive to reduce internal exposure by protecting your mouth and nose with non-polluted towels, etc. along with avoiding intake of water or food suspected of contamination and by stable iodine administration, etc.

Refutation of an A-bombed city

A report of Hiroshima city Sectional Meeting Specialized in Nuking Damage Estimation (2007)
(President Hiromi Hasai, Professor Emeritus of Hiroshima University)

"There is no way to protect citizens from nuclear attack except for prevention of their occurrence whether it is intentional or accidental, which inevitably leads to the only solution, the total abolition of nuclear arms."

Remarks of Hasai, Professor Emeritus of Hiroshima University

"I wonder if Japan's risk of being targeted by foreign attack has suddenly grown nowadays, and if so, what would be the cause? State actors could target Japan because of her alliance with the U.S., which is the world's most powerful nuclear-weapon state, and also for Japan's reliance on the nuclear deterrence of the U.S. for her defense strategy. Non-state actors could target Japan depending on how she deals with the war on terrorism led by the U.S.."

"There is no defense under nuclear attack and avoiding it is the best defense. However, as long as nuclear weapons exist, there is a possibility for them to be used, so their total abolition is the ultimate answer. If Japan chooses to cry out for their abolition as the first victimized nation, it is crucial that Japan gets out of the American nuclear umbrella protection to gain the trust of other countries.

(Hiroshima Peaceful Culture Center bulletin, "Peaceful Culture" October edition 2008)

Remarks of Kazunaga Ito, mayor of Nagasaki city

"It's impossible to protect the public if nuclear weapons are used. If Civil Protection Plan is incorporated casually, it might cause misunderstanding that nuclear damage is minimal."
(at Nagasaki city Civil Protection Council, Jan.31, 2007)

Nagasaki city Disaster Prevention and Crisis Management Office

"While Civil Protection Plan is for each municipality to create tangible measures against A-bombing based on the Japanese government's damage estimation, the national basic guideline is much too far away from the reality of A-bombing damage that A-bombed Nagasaki city deems it unacceptable. In case of A-bombing, the reality is that there is no guarantee for a task force to function and even rescue and relief effort is difficult, let alone evacuation guidance. Moreover, if the personal measures like raincoats and so on are said to be protective against nuclear attack, then its grounds based on facts should be presented. Unless damage estimation of nuclear attack is made under the Japanese government's responsibility, Civil Protection Plan has no realistic effect. As for Nagasaki city, just like Hiroshima city which has made the damage estimation of her own, we hold fast to our assertion that without total abolition of nuclear arms, it is impossible to protect ourselves from nuclear damage. (2014)

HIROSHIMA APPEAL

APPEAL TO LAUNCH A MOVEMENT OF THE WHOLE NATION AGAINST PRODUCTION, POSSESSION AND USE OF ATOMIC AND HYDROGEN BOMBS

Secretariat of Shimonoseki Atomic Bomb Exhibition "Atomic Bombs and Poems of Sankichi Toge"
National Coordinating Committee for the Movement against Atomic and Hydrogen Bombs

The United States of America dropped atomic bombs on Hiroshima and Nagasaki 57 years ago.

These acts are unforgivable crimes against humanity. We demand apology from the U.S. government. It is an important duty that the atom-bombed citizens of Hiroshima and Nagasaki should convey their anguish, grief and anger to the younger generations and peoples in the world to realize world peace. Any element that hampers them from doing their duty should be eliminated. Particularly, it runs counter to the historical truth to call the atomic bombings "merciful acts to end the war" and to regard the citizens enforced horrible death or suffering by the appalling atomic bombs as war collaborators. These claims should be considered to have intentionally been propagated and been deliberately brought into people's mind by the atom-bombers. But the truth is that the U.S. has occupied Japan exclusively after World WarII, has waged wars incessantly, using its military bases in Japan. We can say it is not for the purpose of bringing peace and democracy to Japan and the world that the atomic bombs were dropped.

It is only the U.S. government alone in the history of mankind that has ever thrown atomic bombs, the cruelest weapon of mass slaughter, squarely at the people. The U.S. government actually prepares for the case of using nuclear weapons as preemptive attacks against North Korea, China, Russia, Iraq and some other countries. It produces the most serious and impending danger of nuclear war.

The Japanese government sticks to pro-U.S. policy through and through, supporting the U.S. such as in joining Missile Defense Program. It mentions the possibility of its own nuclear armament and schemes to enact laws in time of war. It is taking the course of making our nation opposed by the neighboring nations to whom Japan once caused a tremendous number of casualties and huge damage during the past wartime, thus isolating Japan from the world. We never allow the Japanese government to lead our nationals to such disgracing conduct which throws other Asian countries as well as our nation again into flames of war and nuclear devastation. There are several nuclear powers in the world, but the nuclear weapons all over the world shall never be abolished unless the U.S. government takes the lead in giving up its nuclear arsenal.

Though public opinion against nuclear weapons is roused in whole Japan and the entire world, the movement to ban the atomic and hydrogen bombs appears to be superficial and to lose its truthful power. That is, we should not accept the tendencies to use the movement only as a tool for the interests of this or that political party, but have to turn it into the activities based on the true voices of atom-bomb devastated survivors, getting out from its narrow limits. To ban the atomic and hydrogen bombs is a desire of all the nation beyond political affiliation, ideology, religion and occupation. This requires that a movement of the whole nation should be launched.

In order to meet that requirement, we have to go back to the starting point of the movement, which Sankichi Toge together with other fighters initiated in Hiroshima in 1950's and developed into a world movement, seeking to ban the atomic and hydrogen bombs in order to realize peace, in defiance of the U.S. military suppression. Its movement had a feature of sincere and heart-felt motives of representing the feelings of the atom-bombed citizens.

The U.S. can not use nuclear weapons as it wishes if we can help the atom-bombed citizens of Hiroshima and Nagasaki to raise their genuine voices, and by inheriting their voices, mobilize young power and encourage the workers to play their role of establishing world peace. Let us unite with the peace-loving people in the world and launch a powerful movement all over the country to stop all the nuclear powers from producing, possessing and using the atomic and hydrogen bombs.

6th August 2002

The Untold Truth of the Great Tokyo Air Raids

Reports of activities in Tokyo by the national caravan for The Atomic Bomb Exhibition entitled "Atomic Bombs and Poems of Sankichi Toge"

Around Diet building burnt down by air raids.

Many elderly people talk about their experiences of the air raids while viewing the panel. (at the JR Machida station)

A grave with names of missing persons carved by the Morishita-5-chome group in Koto-ward.

250,000 citizens were killed or wounded for the purpose of controlling the Greater Tokyo Metropolitan Area

Symposium by the Atomic Bomb Exhibition Caravan 2015 and reporters of the Choshu Newspaper

As many as 130 persistently repeated large-scale air raids

The nationwide indignation against "security related legislations" which evolved into the SDF to fight overseas as the U.S. Army's sub construction has been growing. The indignation has been swelling together with the traditional anger against Japan's dependency towards the U.S. for 70 years after the World War II. All the while our press has sent Atomic Bombs Exhibition Caravans to Tokyo and tried to understand the experiences of Tokyo Major Air Raids and swirling anger among Tokyo residents. Through this grapple, we found that the truth of the Tokyo Major Air Raids is not well known and which is very regrettable. Furthermore, we found that the Tokyo Major Air Raids were a perfect door to Japan's dependent relations with the U.S. today.

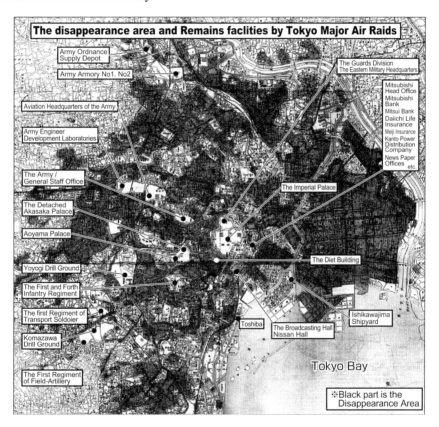

The Imperial Palace, the facilities of financial institutions, military facilities were in perfect condition

Chairperson : In the Atomic Bomb Exhibition Caravan activities in Tokyo, many residents began to pour out their experiences of the Tokyo Major Air Raids. Many people pointed out sharply that no public memorial monuments or memorial halls were built in Tokyo even after 70 years of WWII, in spite that the raids killed 100,000 people over one night, which was an unparalleled disaster in the whole world. We would like to start with the experiences and desperate thoughts of the Tokyo Major Air Raids victims.

A : It is generally said that 100,000 were killed in Tokyo Major Air Raids. From the first air raids in April, 1942, five months after the attack of Pearl Harbor, including the most seriously damaging air raids on March 10th, 1945, until the end of the war, over 130 continually repeated air raids were conducted. The research data of the Tokyo Metropolis reported the number of the dead, the injured, and the missing was 250,670 and the number of the war victims was 3044,197. The toll of the victims is larger-scale than that of Hiroshima and Nagasaki, or the Battle of Okinawa.

It must be emphasized that there has been and will be no such great air raids anywhere in the world as the Tokyo Major Air Raids on March 10th, which killed more than 100,000 citizens within only a couple of hours. Tokyo presented much more terrible sights than Iraq or Syria. Nevertheless, "this tragedy has never been told so far."

B : Whenever we have "Atomic bomb and war exhibition" on the street corners of Tokyo, the experiences of Tokyo Major Air Raids pour out everywhere without exception. A person said, "Our forty-six family members and relatives were killed." Another said angrily, "Why don't we have any memorial monuments even now?" Their rage severely shocked us.

A man who experienced the Air Raids at Asakusa said, "I got involved in the air raids when I came back from my evacuation to attend the elementary school graduation ceremony. Thirty classmates were killed. I ran away crossing the Kototoi Bridge but those who failed to escape were burnt to death. A fire engine was wrapped in flames and its driver turned into a skeleton with his hands holding its steering wheel. Not hundreds but thousands of corpses lay in piles like blue fins."

He insisted, "After the war people were on the verge of starvation. Some foods such as canned corned beef provided by the U.S. Army were distributed. We felt as if we were dogs that were made to take food from humans. But without eating, we would starve to death, so we made a queue to get our food rations. The U.S. regards a Japanese as an insect, nevertheless Japanese power-holders passed a bill that demands us Japanese to die for the U.S.. We still have a deep-seated grudge. Please keep on revealing the truth of the Tokyo Major Air Raids. I hope this exhibition caravan will be held in the middle of Ginza."

C : The sight of Tokyo after the Major Air Raids was as disastrous as those of Hiroshima and Nagasaki after the Atomic Bombings. The U.S. Army arranged the perfect air raids procedure. They decided to conduct the air raids in March, when strong spring winds blow. Oil bombs were developed so that they could burn private houses effectively. The bombs were dropped on the area surrounding the eastern downtown of Tokyo near Tokyo Bay where ordinary private houses stood close together. The area turned into a sheet of flames with no escape routes. The U.S. Army made concentrated attacks and even shot machine guns on the citizens running about in the sea of flames trying to escape.

Many people said, "We cannot forget those laughing pilots who were aiming and shooting machine guns at us." Not only burnt black corpses but also pink suffocated corpses like wax dolls lay scattered. They were piled and burnt in the parks or school grounds. In Kinshi Park, Kinshi-cho, Sumida, they say, about 14,000 bodies were burnt and buried temporarily. But there is not even a single signboard telling what the Air Raids brought about. We hear there were too many bodies to burn at a time, so, for many days, people carried those bodies to the rivers or the sea to throw them away.

On the bridge parapets over the Sumida River and the ground under the Sobu Line railroad, human oil stains still remain as they were when piles of the bodies were burnt. They say the sites have been repainted again and again but the stains still come up to the surface.

As for the air raids on Shinagawa in May, gasoline was sprinkled at midnight and firebombs were scattered. "What can be a worse war crime than these air raids?" many in their seventies and eighties ask. This is not at all an old tale. They have a buildup of grievances all the more because they have had no opportunities to relate their experiences. The so-called 110,000 ashes temporarily buried at parks are now interred at the Memorial Hall for Kanto Great Earthquake victims, Yokozuna, Sumida Ward. There are no memorial facilities which console the Tokyo Major Air Raids victims exclusively. The point is why such is the situation?

"Let people forget the war"
GHQ Rejected the Application for Building War Memorial Monuments in Japan

D : The Residents' Association of Morishita 5-chome Koutou Ward, the place where the Great Tokyo Air Raids caused devastating damage, built a cenotaph in March this year. The names of 789 victims are engraved on it. According to a board member of the neighborhood association, the movement to build this monument was started by the efforts of a remarkable man, a man who had been the president of the residents' association 70 years ago. Immediately after the war, he conducted a detailed survey of the victims of the air raids in the Morishita 5-chome area. He recorded his findings and kept them on a 10 meter long scroll, known as "the wartime death register". He painstakingly scoured the "government bond purchasers' name list" which he had saved from burning, for the victims' names. Thanks to this scroll, the bereaved families' strong desire to erect a memorial to acknowledge the victims' lives was finally realized 70 years later.

E : "The wartime death register" contains a record of an unfortunate family whose entire 12 members were killed. The local people, through the efforts of the residents' association, recognized this fact for the first time recently. Although the Tokyo Metropolitan Government is said to have an official directory of the deceased, it refuses to release this official document to the public, thereby rejecting the bereaved families' application. Moreover, it refused official permission to build a Jizo or a monument commemorating the victims because of the policy of separation between religion and politics. However, by turning a blind eye to construction work, it is believed that permission has been tacitly granted. Subsidies from the Tokyo Metropolitan Government were not forthcoming, so one of the bereaved families established a fund into which many people contributed. Through the funds received, enough was raised to finally complete the cenotaph.

In another similar case, soon after the war, local people tried to build a cenotaph at the foot of Kikukawa Bridge in Sumida Ward, where thousands of people had been killed by the Tokyo Raid. However, their application was also rejected by the Sumida's Ward Office. In Sumida, every time a river embankment maintenance work was carried out, many skeletal remains were unearthed. Being no longer able to tolerate the situation, local people came together and built a Jizo by themselves. A memorial service is held every year at the memorial.

D : One of the bereaved families showed me a copy of an administrative document released by the general manager of the Public Relations Department of the Metropolitan Chief Secretariat in 1947 (Showa 22). That was sent for each administrative personnel; chief cabinet each manager, branch length, chief, word mayor what was written about for establishing plan of the Sumida Park War Memorial Tower by the bereaved families.

"1, We would like to remove the war memories by citizens of Japan.
2, Must not remember the war seeing the war memorial tower. So do not accept to establish the tower."

Firstly, the U.S. occupation army's guiding principles stipulated, secondly it was written "We should obey their policy completely."

That's the surprising fact, it's past more than 70 years after the war, we are still under the press cord.

Subordination structure to the U.S. still continues
The top of the Japanese ruling class was connected with the U.S.

A : Even they slaughtered about 250,000 citizens in Tokyo, on purposely they removed the aim. From this fact, we see their aim.
C : The Imperial Palace is representative. Since the beginning of the war, the U.S. army ordered the pilots "Not to Attack" the Palace which had huge area at the center of Tokyo, also the emperor side had known it. There were not damaged

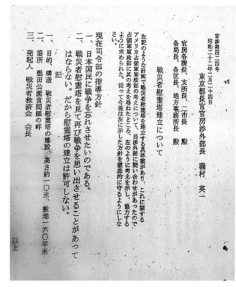

"Do not accept to establish the war memorial tower." An administrative document released by the general manager of the Public Relations Department of the Metropolitan Chief Secretariat (February.24.1947).

where the guards divisional headquarters at the north area of the Imperial Palace, the military nerve center; the Eastern army headquarters, the ministry of war general staff headquarters (ministry of defense) in Ichigaya. There originally had to be attacked.

The detached Akasaka Palace (currently used as a guesthouse), Aoyama Imperial Palace, Shinjuku Imperial Garden, Hama Imperial Villa, Ueno Park… those imperial estates and imperial families' on the bureaucratic machine were completely out of targets. The Tokyo station burned out, but the street of Marunouchi financial buildings caught Imperial palace stayed in the unhurt.

The Mitsubishi head office, Mitsubishi bank. Mitsubishi commercial company, Industrial Bank of Japan, Yokohama Specie Bank, Tokyo Bank, Daiichi Bank, Hypothec Bank, and Kanto Power Distribution Company (Tokyo Electric Power Co.,Inc.) there stand together in large number of financial combine buildings.

News Paper companies such as Asahi and Mainich, Broadcasting

Facing the Imperial Palace by the Tokyo station Yaesu Exit direction. One sees the whole financial district was left on purpose.(1945, Oct)

System Co. Ltd. (NHK) were also left.

Japan Bank, Mitsui head office in Yaesu. The Cabinet Office, House of Parliament, Tokyo Metropolitan Police Department, Department of Interior, Ministry of Finance at Nagatacho and Kasumigaseki were left. Incidentally, the residence of Iwasaki Hisaya, who was the command of the Mitsubishi financial combine, was not attacked as well.

At the Atomic Bombing on Hiroshima, Nagasaki, and at the Shimonoseki air raid, Mitsubishi's main factory had no damages. It proves the friendship between political and business circles and the U.S. This should be specially mentioned, all of the military facilities were left. For example, the heart of the army; Army Armoury in Akabane, Army Magazine, Army Engineer Battalions, Army Head Office of Clothing Depot, Armor Depot, Tokyo First, Second Armor Supply Depot. They were on purposely left in the burnt ground made by attacking. The Imperial Guard Translate Battalion in Yoyogi, Army Translate Regiment Official Residence, the large area of Komaba Drill Ground and the group of official residences of Field-Artillery Corp. All the facilities were no damaged.

E : Even industrial factory, there were not suffer from the attacks where Shibaura industrial complex places Toshiba headquarter offices to port facilities near by Shinagawa station. Thought Ishikawa shipyard, Tajima, Tsukishima adjacent etc... The Shibaura industrial area with the Toshiba head office and the harbor facilities of the neighborhood of Shinagawa Station were not struck, too. Ishikawajima shipyard which was adjacent to the exterminated Fukagawa district and the industrial areas facing Tokyo Bay including Tsukishima etc. are not attacked. In Kamata of the southern part of industrial area where central city area was not burnt down the whole thoroughly, most of the monition facilities such as Haneda airport were not attacked. Industrial aims written down in the Operation duty report of the U.S. Armed Forces are nothing more than 22 places.

It is reported that it was only 18% of those that was destroyed. The Great Tokyo Air Raids was not indiscriminate bombing. It left facilities which would help the rule of U.S. over Japan, and killed the common people who interfered. It was carpet bombing, but sorted targets definitely.

B : Many people told us "Why it was possible for U.S. to carry out such minute bombing in the dark?"

One of those testified that "As a mark to avoid bombing, somebody irradiated light from the ground."

The air raid was not a thing which was unavoidable to end the war. It was a massacre for the purpose of dampening the resistance of the Japanese citizen to occupy Japan exclusively, such as A-bombing.

Murder operation of the U.S. Armed Forces

The Japanese governing classes accepted such murder

A : Tokyo Air Raid has many mysterious points. For example, the precautionary warning was canceled just before the air raid. In the occasion of the A-bombing on Hiroshima and Nagasaki, the precautionary warning was canceled just before the A-bombing. The A-bomb was dropped when everybody went out peacefully. If the center of the military did not cooperate, it was impossible. It was impossible that the Japanese military did not notice the U.S. airplane more than 300. The Japanese military did not do even a proper counterattack permitting the air raid of U.S. Armed Forces. The difference of the amount of resources between Japan and the U.S. was obvious. However, we cannot give a proper explanation about having permitted the air raid of the U.S. without counterattacking it.

War orphan was captured and isolated inside a cage of iron grating following the U.S. army's policy. (July 1946 In Tokyo Water Police Department)

F : When U.S. army dropped the atomic bomb on Nagasaki and Hiroshima, the Japanese army had known beforehand that they were going to attack there using the radar irradiation.

By receiving the signal, the Imperial Headquarters knew that the plane carrying the atomic bomb was near. In Nagasaki, the group that was organized to attack the B29 was waiting at Omura air corps and was ready to fire and was waiting for the command. After everything, there were no commands. NHK also broadcast the scene which the former pilot objected against it angrily.

A : Just before the end of war, the Special Police Force watched over some young officers. That was because the police force feared that they would revolt due to the loss in the war. Although the Leftists were destroyed early, young officers had a fighting experience and the Upper army unit wanted to welcome America quickly to occupy Japanese territory but the young officers had been a threat. Although losing the war was imminent, the Upper army unit insisted upon the citizens to obey "suicide attack of honor by one hundred million people". Young people were forced to do the special operation campaign and they were made to protect Japan at the risk of losing their lives, so they resisted the Upper army force's way to maneuver the end of war quickly. Before the emperor's broadcast about "Imperial Rescript on the Termination of the War", there was an incident involving young officers belonging to the ground forces that tried to kill Division commander Konoe and deprive the sound board. Furthermore, there was also an incident wherein young officers tried to kill Macarthur when he was coming to Atsugi. There is a famous story that Takamatsunomiya, who had been an influence to the young officers depressed these incidents desperately.

B : Just after the war ended, there was disarmament by the army's order in the mainland. That order won't be activated only by the emperor's command. The order can't be carried out without the military headquarters order. To carry out the order, they needed to leave the center of the army before the U.S. army arrives in Japan. Since the beginning, there were many soldiers in the center including the navy that were friendly to the U.S.. Also ground forces got stuck in China and shifted the plan to southern operations. They hadn't sent any food and ammunition although they sent army to the southern islands. A soldier who experienced the battle of New Guinea Front said that they ate potatoes every day. Almost every person died because of hunger and illness.

D : When Japan was defeated, who cooperated with the U.S. landing and single occupation in that chaos? Somebody who cooperated with the U.S. was apparently cleared from the building which was intact. After the war, there was "the dissolution of the zaibatsu", but actually the zaibatsu had been preserved starting with the emperor, who ordered the citizens to begin the war and the Bureaucracy. It was symbolic that Nobusuke Kishi, who was the minister of commerce and industry when the war began, became a CIA agent after the war. He was never criticized by the political world and officials, and helped the U.S. as the collaborator of occupation of Japan after the war. There were also other collaborators as CIA agents in the press like Matsutaro Shoriki who was the former official at the center of the Imperial Headquarters and who worked in the Yomiuri press, and Taketora Ogata, who was also a former official who worked in the Asahi press.

Either in Iraq or Afghanistan, resistance will certainly occur when they try to occupy another country,

The farewell service which sees the family at the site of the fire (1945.May. Tokyo.Kudan)

and whatever years it takes, they will try to defeat the invaders using force. Then why was the U.S. able to occupy the whole country of Japan without resistance? That was because the dominant organization cooperated with the occupation of Japan with the U.S. and they sold their country. The dominant organization that was controlled military by the U.S. as its tool after the war and it continues up to now.

E : All the people who survived the air raid and who lived in the old town went out of the town because they had nothing to eat and couldn't live there after the war. Citizens were scattered so as not to cause any resistance. The air raid thoroughly disabled them in resisting and that caused people in the capital area to live in desperate circumstances such that they weren't sure if they can survive tomorrow. The air raid was dome totally to suppress the capital area and occupied like a Shock Doctrine.

C : Food shortage was terrible after the war because the U.S. army controlled food intentionally. There was a witness who was the former procurement clerk.

He testified that U.S. army controlled internal food storage in Japan and drove the people into a food crisis. The U.S. army made a mine blockade in Kanmon Strait which was called "Operation Starvation". They didn't let Japanese send food to the battlefield from Japan, and that was the hunger strategy in order to shut down the food supply from the continent. There was no food to eat in urban areas. They survived hunger by eating the soybean that was distributed and kept in their pocket, and drank a lot of water.

Although there was starvation and many people died as a result, U.S. sent Lara goods that were feed stuff for animals. The Diet passed a vote of thanks about it. That was a shame.

E : After the war, in the cities of Ueno and Asakusa, there were thousands of children who became orphans and vagrants and were forced into stealing and selling sex in order to survive. The GHQ apprehended these children and sent them to compulsory exile on the pretext of "maintaining public order". It was required by the U.S. Armed Forces that this facility was built on the sea and the children were under constant surveillance so that they could not escape.

B : Although Japan had already demilitarized, the Occupation Forces were still carrying guns, using trams which were only for Americans and banning Japanese people from entering some buildings. This is because "the U.S. Army were afraid of counterattacks by Japanese citizens."

A : For instance, it was known that the number of army personnel amounted to a million when Japan occupied Manchuria. However, it was too few to do so in Japan. It is because, the Japanese governing classes performed substitution politics as U.S. subordinate. It made the U.S. Army control Japan much easier. As we know, it is difficult to suppress a riot by citizens if a hostile army totally ruled there, such as in Iraq and Syria. In contrast, the Japanese governing classes cooperated with the U.S. Army to depend their own positions. It led the U.S. to control Japan easily.

F : In Germany which was also a defeated nation like Japan, all Nazis were banished from there. All newspaper companies also were dismantled. That country had a freedom of independence. This is because Germany concluded a peace treaty with the Allied Powers. It is different in Japan, which was controlled only by the U.S..

When a cold war was finished in 1990s, Germany became independent. The prime minister in Germany advised "Take it easy" to Japan because Japan advanced a direction for strengtning subordination to the U.S.. As a result, Japan is still the subordinate state under the U.S.- Japan Security Treaty.

A : In fact, each of the ministries and government offices which constitutes the bureaucracy, is linked to U.S. such as the Ministry of Finance, Economy and the Defense Agency. The American embassy has a strong power to adopt some strategy in Japan.

For example, Summers, who was the Secretary of the Treasury, made an objection directly to the Ministry of Finance many number of times. Also, U.S. government officers poured into the prime minister's official residence and gave instructions when the Fukushima nuclear accident happened. Mr. Kan, who was the former prime minister, could only follow U.S. instructions about it. In fact, it is impossible to explain the change of prime minister from Mr. Hatoyama to Mr. Kan and Mr. Noda without the involvement of the U.S.. It shows the relationship between Japan and the U.S. as the subordinate state and master until now.

Zaibatsu and Media also tried to keep their positions under the U.S. control

C : One lady, who lived in Akasaka-mitsuke during the war, had a relative who was able to go to the American embassy. She said "there were a lot of policeman in civilian clothes who guarded outside of the building, it looked stern. On the other hand, people inside played golf. That looked calm and confident under the war, as if they had already won it. "

F : When six months had passed after the attack on Pearl Harbor, Clark Grew, who was the American Ambassador to Japan at the time, went back to the U.S. He performed "the court diplomacy", in Japan and deepened a friendship with the attendants of the Emperor, including Kouichi Kido, Aoi Shigemistu, Shigeru Yoshida and Fumimaro Konoe. They were considered "liberalist and moderates" who were in conflict with anti-U.S. factions of Japanese army. Grew worked only six months for making up a program to lead the ending of the war.

He said "No worries" to Mr. Chichibumiya, and went back to the U.S. he said in the U.S. "Do not attack the Imperial Palace. The Emperor was useful for worshipping militarism and will be useful as a symbol as well." He also corresponded with Shigeru Yoshida directly.

Edwin Oldfather Reischauer, who was the American Ambassador to Japan after Grew, was then a secret agent. He made a program which made the emperor act as an American tool for indirect rule over Japan. Under this program, he suggested to the US army that they should constantly transmit important information to about 500 elite Japanese being allowed to listen shortwave broadcasting. In fact, "Zacharias radio broadcasting", which the only upper echelons of society were able to listen, transmitted important information like "When and where U.S. makes air raids." They also knew when atomic bombs were dropped on Hiroshima and Nagasaki.

Koichi Kido, who was one of the attendants, proposed to the Emperor in June that their positions would be guaranteed by being defeated to the U.S.. This is because he knew everything about the attacks from U.S. through the radio.

A : In February, Shigeru Yoshida, who got information from U.S., made Fumimaro Konoe write a report to the Emperor. It says "America and Britain do not require us to change the national polity (the emperor system). What we should be concerned with are mostly occurring communist revolutions along with losing the war rather than losing the war." They were concerned not with victory or defeat but with how to control the

citizens and keep their positions under the American occupation. For this purpose, they resigned themselves to atomic bombs. It is rather convenient for them to burn Tokyo up and make the general public exhausted.

F : The financial world had been in touch with the U.S. from the beginning. Koyata Iwasaki, the leader of Mitsubishi instructed "Don't worry, we are friends with America," when the war started and stated "We can enjoy working from now on," when loed the war. Moreover, at the end of the war, Aiichiro Fujiyama (the Japan Chamber of Commerce and Industry), Gisuke Ayukawa (Nissan Group), Yoshizo Asano (Asano conglomerate) and others had organized an advisers' council of the Cabinet. According to Fujiyama, they announced a plan to recover immediately the economic relationship with U.S. in the conference six days before ending the war. He delightfully said that "Our age has come," and toasted the coming of the new age with a bottle of champagne at a leisure house in Karuizawa. They were sure that U.S. treated them carefully from the beginning. Grue himself was a representation of Morgan conglomerate that was intimately related to Mitsubishi. His main mission was how to protect the interests and properties they had invested since prewar. There were a lot of connections made between Japanese in the financial world and American in Japan such as Ayukawa and Ford, Asano and Roosevelt.

A : An aggressive war toward China reaching a dead end, control centers including the emperor and financial world already knew that Japan would lose. However, their control positions would be lost if China defeated Japan. Therefore,

they started fights with U.S., surrendered to U.S. to protect their positions. They carried out their will that they must sacrifice their citizens to achieve their purposes.

All the parties are pro - American
A desire for power representing the general public

C : Tokyo has all the headquarters of political organizations. However, considering issues of memorial towers there, it does not have any force to meet citizens' demands. First of all, it is because of suppressions and propagandas from U.S. It thoroughly spread propaganda as if it had been a friend of peace and democracy, fought to release Japan, and obliged to drop atomic bombs and air raids to end the war. It also restricted speeches and oppressed the nation more aggressively than during the war. It suppressed speeches leading to anti U.S. such as about the atomic bombs and the Tokyo great air raid.

The other great reason is that the leader of the Communist Party, which should have been on the citizens' side, has not blamed U.S. for its sins like atomic bombs and the Tokyo great air raid though it prescribed "U.S. Forces as a liberation army" and criticized only the former military authorities. Citizens in Tokyo are suppressed by both U.S. and the leader of the Communist Party and were unable to say anything.

B : Citizens accumulated anger toward the Tokyo great air raid. However, even those who were born in Tokyo have little knowledge about it. This is mainly because the reformist power pretended to be as progressive and argued, "Japan should reflect on itself because it attacked Chongqing first. It cannot be helped because it was Japan that caused the war." These are in common with the statement that atomic bombs were "necessary to release from the Japanese Army."

F : The prewar Communist Party was oppressed by the emperor system and brought about its disappearing without any connection with the citizens. It did not reflect on itself but was proud of "18 years in prison". They regarded U.S. as a friend for releasing it while it had despised ordinary people for cooperating with the war. It attacked the former special attack corps and soldiers as "assaulter" and mistakenly reversed the friend and the enemy.

The center of the leadership, Kyuichi Tokuda and others proceeded toward GHQ and gave three cheers for the "liberation army" at the national people's congress right after they were released by the American Army. They thanked MacArthur for "opening democratic revolutions" and stayed long at GHQ to provide him with information about the anti- U.S. movement. Appreciating in such a way for the atomic bombs and the Tokyo air raids in their minds, they would not let us criticize them directly. It also symbolizes the unique structure of oppression that there are a kind of intellectuals who are not able to mention subordination problems toward the U.S..

A : The administrative organization cooperated for the America Press Code for Japan and did not allow us to talk about the Tokyo air raid. Moreover, the Communist Party ignored citizens in Tokyo who met such terrible situations, and regarded U.S. as a friend of peace and democracy. It reversed the friend and the enemy, rather treating the citizens as enemies. That's why they are still indifferent to the Tokyo air raid. It means it did not care about citizens' troubles at all.

C : It is said that American democracy was good, but what have brought about now, 70 years later? Japan has all its wealth exploited and turned into a terrible situation. The U.S. finally came to take our Self-Defense Forces to battlefields without any modesty instead of their own army. Shinzo Abe is cooperating with them actively. The root of the treason politics has not changed at all. The start of the postwar of the Left was mentioned above. There is not a meaning without considering the citizens' hardships, even if they talk about national politics abstractly. To be popular is to be regional and concrete. We cannot see the national universality unless we put a scaffold there. Tokyo has so many headquarters of political parties and most scholars in Japan, none of whom has the power to denounce the U.S. with anger for the tragedy of the Tokyo air raid.

A : The experiences of Tokyo air raid have remained untold. These facts were eliminated intentionally without any single memorial tower. There is a significant difference compared to Hiroshima, on which the atomic bomb was dropped. Hiroshima has the Peace Park, Archives Center and memorial tower. On August sixth, everyone comes to pray from early in the morning because it is the death anniversary of tens of thousands of people. In addition, there are many kinds of memorial towers everywhere in town such as neighborhood associations, schools and companies. What is the difference? It is because Hiroshima has fought. In postwar Hiroshima, the Press Code did not let people talk about

the atomic bomb. The concept that "the A-bombing was an inevitable measure to end the war" vanished the citizens' anger toward them or restricted it thoroughly. However, in those days people talked about it for a long time showing their keloids in public baths. In Hiroshima those behaviors were directly revealed as "It's a crime toward mankind!" and struggles occurred. A struggle on August 6, 1950 was the beginning, which caused a world convention five years later.

It was the Chugoku Region Committee of Communist Party led by its principal Masayoshi Fukuda that instructed this movement, and in those days the Central Committee of the Communist Party also oppressed fights in the Chugoku Region based on the viewpoint that the U.S. Forces is a "Liberation Army". The same structure is still alive in Tokyo: not revealing the enemies on the side of Japanese citizens but regarding the enemies as friends. There was a big difference when they started after the war. It must be clear who is the enemy and who is the friend. It is awful to believe in illusions about the fakes of American democracy. Many Japanese people were killed. The U.S. is the enemy which invaded Japan. Japanese citizens have encountered terrible situations both during the war and postwar. Hatred toward the citizens' enemy and affection toward citizens must be unified. We should stand in the position which represents the citizen while revealing the enemy. Such attitude is also required in Tokyo.

American military dominating the capital

Japanese public opinion about becoming independent was rising up across parties

A : The Greater Tokyo Metropolitan area has the second largest

number of U.S. military bases. The U.S. military bases in Tokyo alone occupy 1,603 hectares, which is equal to the area of 30 Tokyo Domes. Almost all of the areas which were out of the attack target in the major air attack in Tokyo changed into U.S. bases or buildings for the Self-Defense Forces of Japan. The Yokota base is the headquarters of the United States Forces in Japan and a command post to oversee all of the U.S. military in Japan and the Self-Defense Forces of Japan. In Kanagawa prefecture, there is the Yokosuka base as the base of the 7th fleet of the U.S. military having atomic-powered aircraft carriers. Moreover, there are various kinds of buildings and facilities such as the headquarters of the U.S. military, U.S. Army Sagami General Depot where there was an explosion accident, the communications facilities, facilities for storage of fuel, residential areas and places for military exercises.

The Yokota base is the most important one for the U.S. Asian strategy which has a 3350m-long runway and there are approximately 3,400 soldiers, 200 civilian employees of the Department of Defense and about 14,000 people. The base is called "Yokota bakufu" (bakufu means Japan's feudal government.) The base's stock weapons and military supplies were imported from the U.S., Hawaii and so on into the U.S. Army Sagami General Depot, and then, transported from Yokota base by airplane. Under the system, the Yokota base is the base for war supplies, which oversees the western Pacific Ocean and East Asia.

There is also an American base called Akasaka Press Center at Minato city in the heart of the Metropolis close to Roppongi Hills. There are research facilities of land forces(AROME), ONRA-

SIA, offices of "Stars and Stripes", conservation contact detachments, the 78th fleet of Zama base, dormitories for single officers and the Azabu U.S. military heliport in the base. The base plays a role for the American intrusion to Japan by way of the Yokota base. There are no immigration inspection and no regulation such as customs. The base has no obligation to give information about people entering via this base. Even on maps, the area of the base is blank, which means the base is a top secret.

Furthermore, Huchu, Yoshiki, Owada, Ioujima, the transmission facility of Ioujima, New Sanno U.S. military center for the Japan-U.S. Joint Committee (Minato-ku), Tama service center as well as amusement facilities for families of U.S. military are also there. Just after the WWII, 208 U.S. military facilities were in the Tokyo Metropolitan area which was given back because of residents' ardent movement, but substantially each of them can reactivate whenever. The plan of extension of Tachikawa airport which used to be an airport for attacks received a sudden check because of the Sunagawa dispute, and then the airport was returned. The Air Self-Defense Force base is shared by both Japan and America, and the vast government-managed park, base for disaster prevention, roads and playgrounds remained as they were. It is said that they set the regulation of architecture around the area to enable conversion of the roads into runways when necessary. If a war starts, the whole town will change into a military base.

B : Moreover, there is a vast American military airspace above the Greater Tokyo Metropolitan area (Metropolitan Tokyo, Tochigi, Gunma, Saitama, Kanagawa, Niigata, Yamanashi, Nagano, Shizuoka prefectures). The airspace is called "Yokota RAPCON". Japanese civilian airplanes can never go through this airspace under 7,000 m without American military permission. Civilian airplanes departing from Haneda airport or Narita airport must ascend sharply or make a long detour to cross the RAPCON because those airplanes cannot depart normally as other ones do from other airports, which leads to many accidents involving take-off and landing. There are no countries where permission from the American military is needed to fly above the Metropolitan area.

A : On the one hand, Okinawa prefecture is a forward base. On the other hand, the Metropolitan is areas filled with the headquarters. The U.S. captures the whole of Japan by means of dominating the Japanese headquarters. It killed a lot of Japanese people during the Tokyo major air attack and deployed the American military in Japan for the purpose. The matter in Okinawa prefecture is not exceptional. The U.S. causes enemy countries to attack itself first and then make a counterattack like in Pearl Harbor, the Philippines and Vietnam. That's how the U.S. conducts. Tokyo filled with the headquarters is most likely to be the target of missiles.

B : A man who experienced Tokyo major air raid said with anger "It's obvious that America is a problem. However, there are no parties to antagonize it. After all, there are only politicians who betray their own country to save their positions." After the air raid, he applied to join the army as a mechanic and was assigned at the Atsugi airport, but he was just made to dig underground air-raid shelters, and U.S. exploits them now. He said earnestly that he has managed a factory after the WWII. However, if Japan participates in the TPP, all of his jobs will be lost. That's all for America. Such things must be exposed more greately". The people who supported the Liberal Democratic Party doesn't believe the high position politicians, and each citizen keeps his deep thoughts inside.

F : The number of dead people during the Tokyo major air attack is equal to the ones in Hiroshima, Nagasaki and Okinawa combined. The people should hand down the truth from generation to generation, which could become a potent power to shape public opinions and to prevent Japan from being involved in American wars. To achieve that, the Japanese nation needs political forces which listen to the public voice and lead the whole of Japan disregarding their own desires. They are asked to be more open and clarify their enemy and serve the nation.

Chairperson : The security legislation shows that the submissive relationship of Japan with the U.S. essentially threatens Japanese peace. Japan cannot avoid becoming battle fields without confronting this issue. This is the main public voice. Because it is based on the serious experiences of WWII, this voice cross the boundary of the political parties. Our caravan promotes peace activities to hand down this grave experience regardless of political parties, thoughts and creeds. It teach us that based on the serious historic experiences of people and struggling to exalt those experiences, we can develop the peace movement having a magnificent base in the people.

A-bomb Survivors and War Victims Speak Out

Printed on July, 2017

Edited by The Secretariat of the Shimonoseki A-bomb Exhibition
Pablished by The Chosyu Newspaper
Address   10-2, Tanaka-machi, Shimonoseki City,
          Yamaguchi-prefecture 750-0008 Japan

Tel   +81-(0)83-222-9377
Fax   +81-(0)83-222-9399
E-mail   info @ chosyu-journal.jp

All rights reserved. No part of this publication may
be reproduced or transmitted, in any form or by any
means, without the permission of the Publisher.

In the publication of this book, many people cooperated with us. In particular,
college students, graduate students and native English teachers of Hiroshima
University, Hiroshima Shudo University and Yasuda Women's University
helped with translations and editing the English. Without their assistance, the
publication of this book would have been impossible. We deeply appreciate
their valuable contribution.

A-bomb Survivors and War Victims Speak Out

2017年7月7日　　初版第1刷発行

編　集　　下関原爆展事務局
発行者　　森 谷 建 大
発行所　　長 周 新 聞 社
　　　　　〒750-0008　山口県下関市田中町10-2
　　　　　℡ 083-222-9377　FAX 083-222-9399
印　刷　　(株)吉村印刷

定価は表紙裏に表示してあります。
落丁本、乱丁本は送料当社負担でお取り替えいたします。小社宛にお送りください。
本書の無断転写、転載、データ配信は著作権法上での例外を除き、禁じられています。
Printed in Japan ISBN978-4-9909603-2-2